Roshier H. Creecy

A Black Man's Search for Freedom and Prosperity in the Koyukuk Gold Fields of Alaska

by
Margaret F. Merritt, Ph.D.

RDS Publications
Fairbanks, Alaska

Published by
RDS Publications
Fairbanks, Alaska USA
rdspublications@gmail.com

Library of Congress Control Number: 2018961655

Library of Congress Cataloging in Publication Data:
Merritt, Margaret F. 2019
    Roshier H. Creecy
    A Black Man's Search for Freedom and Prosperity in the Koyukuk Gold Fields of Alaska
    Includes references and original historical images

    1. Virginia Ancestry 2. The U.S. Ninth Cavalry
    3. Washington, D.C. 4. Journey to the Klondike 5.
    Dawson 6. Eureka Creek Roadhouse 7. Bound for Alaska
    8. Wild Lake 9. Wiseman 10. Troubling Times

Printed in the United States of America

ISBN 978-0-9828392-3-2

Cover photo: Photo was taken by Joseph V. Strunka from Bluecloud Mountain looking west into the Glacier River drainage, a tributary to the North Fork of the Koyukuk River. Wiseman sits at the eastern base of Bluecloud Mountain.

This book is dedicated to the old gold miners of Wiseman, whose reminiscences of their lives in the Koyukuk region, and of their recollections of Roshier H. Creecy, provide an honest depiction of Alaskan history remote from most of our experiences. When stripped of specifics, their stories reveal universal desires for independence, prosperity and a sense of belonging.

Table of Contents

Author's Preface

The biography of Roshier Harrison Creecy is an educational journey through a reformative and rapidly changing era in America's history. Our understanding of history is shaped by many narratives, told in different times, each with their own subtle perspectives. This narrative is an important contribution to the historical accounts of the Koyukuk gold mining community in the first half of the 1900s because it adds perspective from an African American man and broadens our understanding of that time in the country.

To support the educational aspects of Roshier's story, the narrative is interspersed with sidebars or "grey boxes," which help describe the concepts, people, organizations, towns and living conditions he encountered, and the roles that political, cultural, martial and socioeconomic forces of the times played in his life story.

To support the genealogical and historical record and to verify evidence as far as is known, sources of information, legal and personal documents, images, and transcriptions of taped interviews are cited in a reference section at the end of the book. Reference numbers are unique and are numbered in the order in which they first appear, with subsequent citations of a particular reference retaining its unique number. All unsourced maps are drawn by the author.

When I began to research Roshier's life, I found a man who objected to mistreatment during an era intent on retaining a racial hierarchy. As I dug deeper into his life and the time he lived in, I realized that the societal obstacles Roshier encountered one hundred years ago, and his strategies to circumvent them, are present for men of color today, supporting William Faulkner's axiom, "The past is never dead. It's not even past." While the obstacles may have transformed from overt to covert over the past century, race is still a matter of conversation.

Born in 1866, Roshier was in the first generation of African Americans who were free to migrate to new regions. His particular fork in the road from Virginia to the Klondike gold fields, which led him to prospect for gold in the remote upper Koyukuk region of Alaska, adds adventure to his story. Roshier was not the first African American to prospect for gold in the Koyukuk. For example, Andy Kuhne was a member of a group of stampeders who arrived in 1898 at the mouth of the Yukon River, bound for the gold fields above Arctic City.[1] However, Roshier was the only African American to spend thirty years in the upper Koyukuk. In the Arctic, Roshier sought freedom to wander, to express himself and to direct his destiny—all of which he achieved. He also sought a quick path to prosperity, but the big gold strike eluded him, as it did for so many others.

Growing up in Rustburg, Virginia, Roshier was known by his family as "outspoken, fearless and aggressive. Roshier did not stand mistreatment."[2] He ran away from home and joined the U.S. Army's Ninth Cavalry, a "colored" regiment known as the "Buffalo Soldiers." Assigned to Company M and stationed primarily at Fort Duchesne, Utah, their mission was to secure the frontier and ensure law and order. Roshier and his regiment became unwitting tools of politicians who justified conflict with Native Americans under Manifest Destiny. Commanding officers of the black soldiers were white. One white officer stated he was "no admirer of the African" but admitted that his service with the Buffalo Soldiers had led him to "think the world of the men in my company. When I look at them I do not see their black faces, I see something only beyond . . . They are far ahead of white troops."[3] During his time in the army the spelling of Roshier's surname changed from "Creasy" to "Creecy."

Following his honorable discharge, Roshier married, had a son named Nathan, and settled in Washington, D.C., where "Jim Crow" laws were less restrictive than other southern cities. But Roshier chafed at the indignities of daily life in a white-dominated culture. With news of the Klondike Gold Rush in 1898, Roshier resolved to join the stampede and quietly slipped away from moral obligation.

Landing in Skagway, Alaska, Roshier stepped into the territory of the notorious Soapy Smith and his gang. He endured three months of treacherous winter travel over the White Pass into the Klondike. Once in Dawson, Yukon Territory, Canada, he prospected, gambled, and became the owner of a roadhouse in Eureka where the North-West Mounted Police billeted. As business waned with increasing stampedes to Alaskan gold fields, in 1906 Roshier mushed his dog team on the Yukon River Winter Trail to Fairbanks, Alaska. From there he headed north to the upper Koyukuk country where he remained the rest of his life. In the remote Arctic mining camps near Wild Lake and Wiseman, he was generally well-liked by his friends and distant neighbors. "Everybody liked Creecy, he got along with everybody. He'd just give you a Creecy story."[4] Roshier was described as "unique, a real character, a good entertainer, always ready to tell a yarn or two, witty, a jokester, a wanderer, hard working, prolific reader, a loner who stayed to himself."[5]

In the Arctic, Roshier found a place and people that were antithetical to the racial discrimination found Outside (the lower 48 states). The Arctic sheltered him from ominous events of the times, such as lynchings of African Americans in the southern and border states, the devastation wrought by two world wars, and the Great Depression. Roshier acknowledged his African American ancestry with a wry sense of humor, spiced with passive-aggressive whispers. When a Wiseman miner who hailed from Alabama asked him how he was doing, Roshier replied with a big grin, "Oh fine, I've got three white men workin' for me."[6]

The peripheral story of Roshier's son, Nathan, who briefly re-entered his father's life at Wild Lake, from 1917–1919, provides another portal into the family's navigation through the early twentieth century. In an interview conducted with Nathan in 1978, he related unvarnished details into a pioneer miner's life as father and son searched for gold in the Alaskan wilderness. Whereas Roshier embraced the isolation of the Koyukuk and retained his African American heritage among his acquaintances, Nathan rejected this strategy. Instead, Nathan left the wilderness for American society where, as a light-skinned African American, he passed as white by substituting his black identity for an Italian lineage.

Roshier's wanderings may have been prompted by the search for prosperity and independence from social restrictions, but his journey led him to discover personal growth and a sense of belonging in a wondrous wilderness hinting of gold.

Acknowledgments

Joseph V. Strunka, Ph.D., a placer gold miner on Nolan Creek, near Wiseman, Alaska, was a major source of information about Roshier H. Creecy. Joe arrived in Fairbanks, Alaska in the summer of 1962 at age twenty-five. He had begun his Master's studies in the fall of 1961 at Eastern Illinois State Teacher's College—Charleston, majoring in geography with a minor in geology. A classmate, who had made several trips to Alaska seeking employment so he could fund his studies the following year, inspired Joe to head to Alaska with the intent of working two months, then returning to college. Having but $195 in cash, Joe traveled from Chicago to Seattle, reached the turn off to Fort St. John, and began hitchhiking the Alaska-Canada Highway. He arrived in Fairbanks with $34 in his pocket, not knowing a soul in town.

After a short "pick and shovel job," he was hired to do gold mining assessment work for an old Klondiker, Robert "Bobby" Henry Jones, and Charles "C.K." Kenneth Harvey. Bobby used a cane and crutch to get around at age seventy-nine; he lived alone on Nolan Creek during summer and in Wiseman during winter. C.K. was in his early sixties and lived in Fairbanks where he worked for Wien Airlines. The two old gold miners welcomed young Joe onto the work-force. The placer mining claims were located on Nolan Creek, 7 miles northwest of Wiseman, Alaska. In 1962, the permanent population of Wiseman totaled eight people: old miners Harry

Leonard, Vincent Knorr, Oliver Chappelle and Wes Ethington; and, two elderly Inupiaq couples, Jacob and Kulhopek Jonas, and Arctic John and his wife, Esther.

Bobby asked Joe if he would care to "split-the-grub" bill and stay with him on Nolan Creek to mine for gold during the winter. Joe, not having a job in Fairbanks and not enough money to go back to school in Illinois, accepted the offer and spent the winter of 1962 through the summer of 1963 living in a 12' x 14' log cabin on Nolan Creek. For Joe, it was a "once in a lifetime opportunity." In addition to placer mining, Joe learned to drift mine underground using steam from a wood-fired boiler, thawing frozen ground to follow the pay streak of gold.

During his time on Nolan Creek, Joe heard many stories from old-timers about the characters of Wiseman's past. One man's name, in particular, kept coming up: Roshier Creecy. Joe became intrigued with the colorful tales about Roshier and wanted to find out more about him. Joe tracked down five old-timers who knew Roshier and tape-recorded interviews with them. He discovered Roshier's great-niece, Loma Pointer, living in Detroit, Michigan as well as Roshier's son, Nathan Cristini, living in Reno, Nevada, and tape recorded interviews with them. In addition, Joe initiated searches for archival information. But life got in the way and the information about Roshier sat in a cardboard box for thirty-five years, until Joe handed the box to me, requesting that I use the information to form the basis of a book. Joe's wish was to educate readers about the life and times of early placer gold miners in the Koyukuk, as experienced through one of the region's more unique characters.

I greatly appreciate Joe's enthusiastic chronicling of memories from the old-timers of Wiseman which reveals vivid details about what it was like to live and mine for gold in the upper Koyukuk nearly one hundred years ago. Special thanks to Vivian Bell with Yukon Archives. The help of Angharad Wenz with the Dawson City Museum and Angela Schmidt with the University of Alaska Archives is also appreciated. I am grateful for the insightful comments offered by Drs. William Schneider and Chris Allan, and Ms. Laura Lund. Many thanks to all the people who made available their historical and genealogical information by publishing and distributing it to lending libraries and posting it on various sites on the internet.

From left: Bobby Jones, Arctic John and Joe Strunka. Photo was taken in December 1964 by Richard C. Henderson of Fairbanks, Alaska at Bobby's two-room cabin in Wiseman, Alaska, previously owned by Hughie Boyle.

Chapter 1

Virginia Ancestry

The June grass smelled sweet, blades tall and knife edged as the two children made their way toward the cows chewing determinedly in the waning light. It was time to bring the cows back to the barn for the night. Twelve year-old Virginia leaped on an old cow's back and the creature half-heartedly tried to shake her off. Virginia's brother, Roshier, who was two years older, laughed. "I'll race you to the gate," he said as he straddled a bony cow. The year was 1880, and the children were the closest of seven remaining siblings who lived with their father, Wyatt Creasy, and step-mother, Silvia, on their small farm in Rustburg, Campbell County, Virginia.[2] The nearest big town was Lynchburg, 12 miles to the north, where they got their mail.

Roshier's father, Wyatt, had been born a slave in Campbell County, Virginia in 1832, a son of his white master, George Clairborne Creasy (1812–1886), and black slave mother, Usley Rosser.[7, 8] George farmed tobacco on 600 acres of land near the Lynchburg and Salem Turnpike, 10 miles south of Lynchburg.[9] In the 1860 U.S. Census, George stated his net worth was $8,800: $6,000 in land and $2,800 in livestock.[10] The Creasy family was among the first settlers in the area, first called Bedford County, which became Campbell

1

County in 1782. Two Creasy forefathers served in the colonial military during the American Revolutionary War.[9]

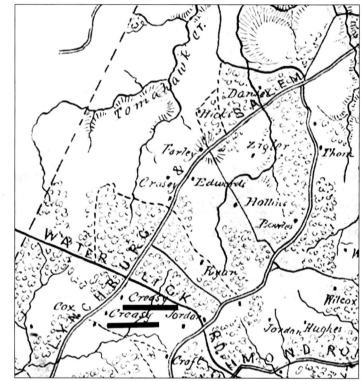

Confederate Army map (1861–1865) of landowners and critical features in Campbell County, Virginia showing George Creasy's land (underlined)[11]

Like many slave-holders of his era, George had two families—one white and one black. In 1831, George married Malinda Arthur and they had seven children: Lillian Ann born in 1832, Thomas Clairborne born in 1839, Gustavus "Gus" Adolphus born in 1840, Sallie Tucker born in 1841, Emily Malinda born in 1849, Robert H. born in 1851, and Grace Jane born after 1851.[12] George's mating with his slave, Usley, occurred around the same time as his marriage with Malinda. The two Creasy families lived side by side on the same farm, interacting with each other in a curious antebellum harmony.

As Wyatt's great-granddaughter Loma Pointer recalled from stories handed down from her grandmother Virginia, "Wyatt talked about the goodness of his master; he was a very good man." George taught his slave son, Wyatt, the trade of carpentry. George also taught Wyatt how to read and write, which was risky, because under Virginia law, it was illegal for a slave to be taught to read and write.[13] In turn, Wyatt made sure his children could read and write and encouraged them to be industrious. Wyatt's daughters were taught to be seamstresses. "You weren't supposed to be idle," said Loma.[2]

In 1860, at age twenty-eight, Wyatt married first Selena, who was about fifteen years old at the time of their marriage.[14] Their first child, Bettie, was born a slave in 1860. Onset of the Civil War in 1861 forced upheaval in the Creasy family's plantation life. Wyatt's two half-brothers, Thomas and Gus, enlisted as soldiers in the Confederate Army, Company C of the Virginia Infantry. It was not until 1864 that Wyatt was conscripted into Confederate service. Many plantation owners were reluctant to supply the Confederate Army with slaves because their labor was needed on the farm and it was unlikely the owners would ever see their slaves again, due to war-related death, injury, illness or escape. With Confederate manpower dwindling, in 1864 the Confederate Congress passed an act to increase the efficiency of the army by employing slaves. Landowners were ordered to make their slaves available for duty.[15] Wyatt was enlisted into a "colored" company in the Virginia Infantry. The duties of his company were to construct breastworks as defensive fortifications

3

around the strategic city of Richmond and Drewry's Bluff, repeated targets of the Union Army. The breastworks were hastily assembled from posts, logs or fence rails and dirt, thrown up to about chest height to provide protection to soldiers firing from behind.[16, 17] All three Creasy brothers (Thomas, Gus, and Wyatt) were engaged at the Battle of Drewry's Bluff, where Thomas and Gus sustained injuries.[9] Wyatt remained in the Confederate Army until surrender in 1865.[8]

Half-brothers Wyatt Creasy (left) and Thomas Creasy (right) fought in the Confederate Army against Union forces at Drewry's Bluff.[9]

Following surrender of the Confederacy, the emancipation of slaves in Virginia in 1865 did not grant them equality, however certain restrictions were lifted; for example, the African American man could now acquire land and vote. Loma proudly recalled that her great-grandpa Wyatt "was one of the first black men in Campbell County to vote."[2]

1. What is your name? *Wyatt Creasy*
2. What is your age? *89* years
3. Where were you born? *Campbell C.*
4. How long have you resided in Virginia? *All my life*
5. How long have you resided in the City or County of your present residence?
6. In what branch of the service were you
7. What service did you render?
8. Under whose order or by whom

9. Who was your master at the time of the War between the States?
10. When did you begin such service? *1864*
11. Where did you begin such service?
12. When and why did you leave the service?
13. Where do you reside? If in a city, give street address. Postoffice *Lynchburg VA R.F.D #2 Box 2.B* County of *Camp...* Virginia
14. What is your occupation for earning a livelihood?

Wyatt Creasy's application for a Civil War pension at the age of eighty-nine [8]

Using meager wages earned as a laborer from his former master and father, as well as wages awarded for serving in the Confederate Army, Wyatt rented 55 acres of land to farm near Rustburg, Virginia where he and Selena had seven more children: Andrew Target born in 1865, Roshier Harrison born in 1866, Letitia Jane born in 1867, Mary Virginia (called "Virginia") born in 1868, Cornelia born in 1870, Usley Annie born in 1872 and Vashti C. born in 1878.[14, 18] Shortly after Vashti was born in 1878, Selena died at age thirty-three, leaving Wyatt with a farm to work and seven children to care for. Bettie, at age eighteen, had left home.[14] Wyatt remedied his woeful situation by marrying second Silvia Mathews on May 21, 1879 in Campbell County, Virginia.[19] At the time of their marriage, Wyatt was age forty-one and Silvia was age sixteen. In 1886, Silvia gave birth to a daughter, India.[20]

Wyatt and his family worked hard to cultivate crops on the farm. In the 1880 U.S. Selected Federal Census for Agriculture, Rustburg Municipality, Campbell County, Virginia, Wyatt Creasy stated on June 2 that he "Conducts this farm" and he "Rents for fixed money rental."[10] At the time, there were three types of land tenure: men could own land, rent their land for a fixed amount of money, or rent their land for a share of the products, otherwise known as "sharecropping." While most of Wyatt's neighbors owned their farms, there were a few in 1880, like Wyatt, who rented for a fixed amount. The pressure was on to produce enough food for his large family, as well as surplus to sell, so he could pay the rent. The agricultural census in 1880 provided the following details: Wyatt had 5 acres in tilled land; 1 acre in permanent pasture, orchard or vineyard; 7 acres in unimproved woodland and forest; and 42 acres in other unimproved land including old fields. He owned one horse, two milk cows, one pig and five chickens. Wyatt estimated the farm value for land and buildings was $100; farming implements were valued at $40; and livestock were valued at $30. His estimated value of all farm production in 1879 was $182. In 1879, Wyatt paid a total of $3 for two weeks of hired labor. Wyatt produced the following on his farm in 1879.[10]

Commodity	Amount
Indian corn	75 bushels
Oats	45 bushels
Wheat	32 bushels
Irish potatoes	5 bushels
Sweet potatoes	2 bushels
Apples	10 bushels
Tobacco	1,200 pounds
Cut wood	30 cords

Wyatt was reputed to be a quiet, thoughtful man, as explained by Loma, who was compared to her great grandfather while growing up. Her mother would say to her, "You are just like grandpa [Wyatt Creasy]. You could ask him something and it would take him so long to answer that you would have forgotten the question."[2]

Although Wyatt's children grew up free, the Reconstruction Era was a confusing and challenging time. African Americans had new opportunities and mobility, but the post-war Virginian economy had collapsed, infrastructure was damaged and many in the defeated Confederacy were determined to retain a racial hierarchy by passing Jim Crow laws to deprive African Americans of newly found civil rights. Wyatt's children rejected the notion that black people were not worthy of equal treatment and justice. Loma explained that her grandmother Virginia and Roshier "were people who were outspoken, fearless and aggressive. Roshier did not stand for mistreatment." In a family story passed down to Loma, Wyatt warned his new wife, Silvia, not to water down the buttermilk she served to the family because he wanted his children to have plenty of good food. Despite the warning, when Silvia served buttermilk Roshier could tell it was diluted. Indignant, Roshier threw the watered-down milk in Silvia's face![2]

Wyatt Creasy and his five oldest daughters, circa 1890[21]

On the brink of manhood, Roshier decided he could not live under dominion from his family or post-war Virginian society. There was no legacy for him to inherit—only hard

8

scrabble farm work. The only way to change his fortune was to change his situation. "Uncle Roshier ran away from home when he was young and they [the family] didn't know where he was for a long time," recalled Loma.[2]

Roshier went to Washington, D.C., a city that drew many African Americans because it had been pro-Union during the Civil War and also because it was a place of vibrant life. He found there an active recruitment of young African American men into the U.S. Army to serve in colored cavalry regiments, known as the Buffalo Soldiers. These regiments were engaged in the Indian Wars to secure the western frontier. On May 10, 1887, Roshier enlisted as a private in the U.S. Ninth Cavalry, assigned to Company M. His enlistment form recorded that he had brown eyes, black hair, mulatto complexion and stood at 5 feet 6.5 inches tall.[22] On November 14, 1887, Roshier and nineteen other recruits assigned to Company M arrived at Casper, Wyoming on the Fremont, Elkhorn and Missouri Valley Railroad, where they were picked up by a horse-drawn wagon and conveyed to Fort Washakie, Wyoming.[23]

Chapter 2

The U.S. Ninth Cavalry

At the end of the Civil War, the U.S. government turned its attention to the West and instituted a policy that forced Native Americans to either assimilate into American society or remove themselves onto reservations where they were to live peacefully. Raids between warring native nations were not tolerated. It was the job of the U.S. Army to subdue these nations by constructing a series of military forts across the frontier, resettle Native Americans onto reservations or "agencies" and pursue armed bands of warriors who objected to resettlement. The purpose of this policy was to ensure the safety of miners, trappers, ranchers and settlers intruding on tribal lands as they moved west. Conflict with native peoples over jurisdiction of land and resources was justified by politicians with the conviction of Manifest Destiny.

Manifest Destiny was a nineteenth-century concept rooted in three main beliefs: 1) Anglo-Saxon Americans and their institutions are virtuous and exceptional; 2) it is the mission of the United States to remake the West into an American image; and, 3) it is a divine duty to accomplish dominion of the West. While Manifest Destiny was never a written policy, the idea of expanding American settlement was felt by early Americans as a kind of romantic self-identity.

However, this concept of the American identity was contested by some prominent citizens of the time, such as Abraham Lincoln and Ulysses S. Grant. Despite its opponents, Manifest Destiny was used to promote expansionism, such as the annexation of the Republic of Texas in 1845 because "it is our manifest destiny to overspread the continent allotted by Providence for the free development of our multiplying millions." Manifest Destiny led to the occupation and annexation of Native American land, especially with the 1862 Homestead Act. This act encouraged hundreds of thousands of families to settle the west on land purchased by the United States through treaties with tribal leaders. The historian Francis Parkman wrote in 1851 that native people were "destined to melt and vanish before the advancing waves of Anglo-American power, which now rolled westward unchecked and unopposed." Remnants of Manifest Destiny ideology remain in twenty-first-century America, such as the belief that it is the mission of the United States to expand, promote and defend democracy throughout the world.[24]

By the time Roshier joined the army in 1887, many military forts had been constructed across the Great Plains, Rocky Mountains and Southwest, a multitude of Indian Wars west of the Mississippi had been fought, and most Native Americans resettled onto reservations. Only a few battles occurred between the army and Native Americans during the last decade of the 1880s.

Thus, Roshier mustered into military service with the Ninth Cavalry at a relatively peaceful time, compared to that regiment's previous history. It was during his time in the army that the spelling of Roshier's surname became "Creecy."

11

Comanche Wars (1836–1877)	Navajo Wars (1849–1866)	Yavapai Wars (1861–1875)
Snake War (1864–1869)	Hualapai War (1865–1870)	Modoc War (1872–1873)
Apache Wars: Jicarilla (1849–1855) Tonto (1871–1875) Victorio (1879–1880) Geronimo (1881–1886)	Ute Wars: Battle at Fort Utah (1850) Walker (1853–1854) Tintic (1856) Black Hawk (1865–1872) White River (1879)	Sioux Wars: First (1854–1856) Powder River (1865) Red Cloud (1866–1868) Great Sioux (1876–1877) Ghost Dance (1890–1891)
Cayuse War (1847–1855)	Paiute War (1860)	Nez Perce War (1877)
Bannock War (1878)	Crow War (1887)	Battle of Sugar Point (1898)

Examples of Indian wars west of the Mississippi in the last half of the nineteenth century (1850–1900)[25]

The **Ninth Cavalry** was one of two segregated regiments of the U.S. Army authorized by Congress in 1866 for black enlisted men who were seeking work and purpose after the Civil War. The soldiers enlisted for five years and received $13 a month, a good wage compared to civilian work available during the Reconstruction Era.[26] The Ninth Cavalry was composed of recruits from the South, initially headquartered in Louisiana, while the Tenth Cavalry was composed of recruits from the northern states. Initially, white officers were placed in command of the black soldiers. Over time, black men rose in rank to become officers.[27]

The nickname, Buffalo Soldiers was given to the soldiers by Native Americans, however there are differing stories regarding the name's origin. One source claims that Cheyenne warriors gave them a name that translated to "wild buffalos" out of respect for their fierce fighting ability. In another story, the Apache gave them this name because "they had curly, kinky hair like bison."[28]

The Ninth Cavalry's first deployment was to Texas in 1867, where their mission was to provide security by means of constructing and maintaining forts. Regular patrols from the forts canvased the surrounding countryside for cattle thieves and homesteaders upsetting law and order. Often, soldiers were assigned to accompany mail, stagecoach and wagon train supply shipments to protect against outlaws, Mexican bandits, revolutionaries and hostile renegades.

Fort Washakie

Roshier found Fort Washakie in a valley at 5,500 feet in elevation on the east bank of the Little Wind River, Wyoming Territory. He had never seen such wild and rugged beauty. Fort Washakie had been established in 1869 as Camp Augur, renamed Camp Brown, and finally renamed in 1878 after Chief Washakie of the Shoshone nation, who was instrumental in leading Shoshone and Bannock peoples into treaty with the United States

Chief Washakie[29]

at the Fort Bridger Treaty Council, establishing the Shoshone and Bannock Indian Agency on 3 million acres in Wyoming's Wind River region.[30]

The Shoshone Indian Reservation (or Agency), was situated at one end of the 9-mile long valley, while the fort was located near the valley's center. In 1876, there were about one thousand Shoshone and six hundred horses on the agency. An article published in the *Cheyenne Weekly Leader* on August 17, 1876 described the fort and environs. "The climate of this valley is most delightful both in winter and summer. In the winter very little snow falls and it generally remains but a few hours. The high mountains surrounding keep the storms from coming into the valley and often present a beautiful sight."[31]

Roshier was fortunate to be assigned to Company M, under the command of Captain Louis H. Rucker. Capt. Rucker, an officer in the Civil War, was rewarded with a commission in the Ninth Cavalry. He was "one of the exemplary company commanders in the Ninth Cavalry....a low key officer whose lower rate of troop desertion and dishonorable discharge reflected his effectiveness."[3] More importantly, he treated his enlisted men fairly. The troop's second lieutenant, John H. Alexander, arrived at Fort Washakie on March 22, 1888, transferred from Fort Robinson, Nebraska. John Alexander, a son of escaped slaves, was among the first African Americans to graduate from West Point and become an officer in the U.S. Army. His first assignment was to the Ninth Cavalry.[32] The men under his command admired his leadership and determination to master tactics and skills amid the unease and outright prejudice against him from his fellow white officers.[3, 32] The Ninth Cavalry had competent officers which helped develop effective troops and win grudging respect from white soldiers. In 1887, a white officer penned a letter to the *Army and Navy*

Journal stating he was "no admirer of the African" but admitted that his service with the Buffalo Soldiers had led him to "think the world of the men in my company. When I look at them I do not see their black faces, I see something only beyond. . . .They are far ahead of white troops."[3]

Chief Washakie (standing left with arm extended) and Shoshone native people confer at Fort Washakie, Wyoming, while cavalrymen look on, 1892.[29]

Training at Fort Washakie included shooting, marching, riding, and mounted and unmounted saber drills. Roshier and the rest of Company M performed "ordinary garrison duties." Garrison life could be boring; much time was spent in drills and caring for their horses and equipment. Beans, coffee, flour and bacon were the staples. A herd of beef cattle was kept to supply meat. Soldiers were issued the model 1873 Springfield rifle and noncommissioned officers were allowed the Colt .44 revolver. Roshier was able to distinguish himself in one important area—he could read and write. Most of the recruits were illiterate due to southern laws forbidding education of slaves.

On June 11, 1888, the troop was ordered to Fort Duchesne, Utah. "In compliance with Order no. 39, troop left Ft. Washakie, Wyoming on June 11, 1888 en route to Ft. Duchesne, Utah where it arrived June 27. Distance marched 302 miles."[33] Transfers of men, companies or entire regiments between the many forts, camps and posts within the military administrative district called the Department of the Platte, were common. The Department of the Platte headquartered in Omaha, Nebraska, encompassed Iowa, Nebraska, Wyoming Territory, Utah Territory and the southern portion of Idaho, overseeing the route pioneers followed west.

Fort Duchesne

In mid-summer 1888, the soldiers of Company M marched onto a plateau in the Uinta Basin in 90°F heat and found dry, rocky terrain that only saw 6 inches of rain annually. Cactus, sagebrush, greasewood, creosote bush and the occasional yucca plant dotted the landscape, in stark contrast to the floral meadows with pine and aspen stands in the Wind River Valley they had left behind. Construction of Fort Duchesne was begun two years earlier to quell an outbreak of inter-band warfare among the Ute native peoples of Utah. The Ute people divided themselves into three bands—the Uinta, the White River and the Uncompahgre. The War Department spent $22,000 to build Fort Duchesne, which was completed in late 1887. Laid out in a horseshoe shape, the fort consisted of officer quarters, enlisted men's barracks, a commissary, hospital, chapel, cemetery, garden, and stables with a parade ground in the center.[3] The fort overlooked the Uinta River. A bridge across the river connected the fort by road to the nearest town, Vernal. Low walls protected the fort on the north, south and west sides, while the river bordered the east side. In addition to two companies of cavalrymen, Fort Duchesne housed four companies of infantrymen with an average detachment of 250 men.[34] The mission of Fort Duchesne was to guard the Indian frontier in eastern Utah, western Colorado and southwestern Wyoming. An article written in *The Salt Lake Herald* stated, "There are 1,000 Uinta Utes at the White Rock Agency north of Fort Duchesne, and 1,500 Uncompahgres on their reservation to the south. There has always been open hostility between these tribes and all that has kept them from open outbreak has been the military at the fort."[35]

Members of the Ute people with Lieutenant Styer of the U.S. Army near Fort Duchesne, Utah, 1886[29]

After just five weeks at Fort Duchesne, Roshier and his fellow soldiers in Company M received orders to undertake another march. "The troop left post, Ft. Duchesne, Utah, Aug. 9, 1888, and marched to Camp Strawberry Valley, Utah for one-month encampment. Distance marched 90 miles."[33]

Cavalry maneuvers at Camp Strawberry Valley, Utah, August 1888[36]

In August 1888 the first camp of its kind, designed to provide instruction "for the purpose of giving the soldiers some realistic training in the field,"[36] was established. It was located in a place called Strawberry Valley, Utah. About 650 men from forts within the Department of the Platte were gathered in this place for training. Roshier saw companies of the Sixteenth and Twenty-First Infantry and Fifth Artillery from Fort Douglas, Utah. Companies of the Fourteenth and Twenty-First Infantry from Fort Bridger, Wyoming Territory joined his company from the Ninth Cavalry, as well as the Sixteenth Infantry from Fort Duchesne, Utah. The men from the various companies trained together in maneuvers, simulating how infantry, artillery and the cavalry would work together in battle.[36] After a month of camping and training on the hot and dusty valley floor, Roshier was relieved to march with his company back to the fort. "Left Camp Strawberry Valley, Utah Sept. 13, 1888, proceeded to Ft. Duchesne, Utah its proper station, where it arrived Sept. 18. Distance marched 90 miles."[33]

Roshier returned to performing ordinary garrison duties including regular patrols to block the Utes from slipping off the reservation to their old hunting grounds in Colorado.[3] The soldiers found several forms of activity and entertainment to break the tedium of garrison duties. They looked forward to shooting practice (on and off horseback), and competed for sharpshooter awards. During off-duty time, Roshier discovered a fort school, where illiterate men were taught to read and write, and a library. An avid reader, Roshier frequented the library to peruse an impressive collection of newspapers, journals and books. Fort Duchesne listed 790 works of miscellaneous literature in its library.[37] A few wives at the fort arranged periodic music performances at the chapel for the men, which were widely attended.[3]

Two other activities entertained the men—playing in a band and participating in sports. Fort Duchesne had a multi-racial music band that played stringed and brass instruments.[3] The band played the evening dress parade when the colors were lowered and offered outside concerts during fair weather. The band was especially popular with local settlers during holidays, such as the Fourth of July. Several members of the Ninth Cavalry had learned to play instruments while at Fort Washakie and brought their enthusiasm for music with them to Fort Duchesne.[37] The troops enjoyed contests in boxing, baseball and running. While there was racial separation during the boxing matches, white and African American soldiers competed together during the baseball and track events.[37]

In January 1889, Roshier and nineteen others, along with teamsters who drove the mule teams, were posted to "Saw Mill," a logging camp located 40 miles northwest of the fort in the Uinta Mountains. This camp had been established in the pine-timbered mountains surrounding the basin to provide rough-cut lumber for construction of fort buildings. Periodically, men were dispatched to cut lumber and send loaded wagons back to the fort.[36] Roshier's experiences at Saw Mill—felling trees, cutting lumber, building and living in a log cabin in the snowy forest—would later help him thrive in the Alaskan wilderness. An additional routine posting of the men was to the "Lime Quarry," where the troops mined limestone.

Across the Uinta River from Fort Duchesne, the soldiers kept a watchful eye on a mining frenzy that had developed around a black substance called "Gilsonite," a form of solid petroleum. The substance was named after an early prospector, Samuel Gilson, who brought it into production after hearing about it in 1868. Native Americans had brought the black substance to a blacksmith who was looking for coal. Instead, the black substance melted. Sam Gilson found many uses for Gilsonite, such as paint, varnish, and an automobile fuel called "Gilsoline." Miners used pick and shovel to loosen the black clumps from the soil, then hoisted the ore from vertical shafts with burlap bags. The work was hard and dangerous, as Gilsonite dust was explosive. Wagon loads were hauled on the Nine Mile Road to Price, where it was loaded onto the train, selling for $80 a ton in 1888. The community that erupted around the black veins, called the Duchesne Strip, was under uncertain jurisdiction. The Duchesne Strip became home to saloons, brothels and gambling houses where fights broke out often among the drunken residents. The town was off limits to the soldiers, who nonetheless circumvented the post guard by swimming across the river.[38, 39] The mining of Gilsonite near the fort was Roshier's first acquaintance with mineral prospecting. He filed away his observations in the back of his mind, not realizing that most of his remaining adult life would be spent prospecting, but for a mineral of another color.

In February 1889, Roshier was sent on a detail to bring horses to the fort. "On February 10, 1889 in compliance with Order no. 25, post 2nd Lt. J. H. Alexander with five enlisted men of troop left post and proceeded to Price to bring 13 newly assigned horses to the post. Returned to post with horses February 17. Distance marched 170 miles."[33] The army had made Price Station a supply point of the Rio Grande Railroad, so the soldiers regularly made the 170-mile round trip to Price to pick up supplies for the fort.[40] Roshier was assigned to undertake this trip several times during 1889. Years later, Roshier recounted tales of his horseback excursions while stationed with the army in Utah, including this story as told to Harry Leonard: "I was out at night on horseback and something appeared suddenly on the trail in front of me. I shot at it and went back the next morning to find a dead cow lying on the trail."[5]

During 1890, Roshier continued to be assigned to postings at Saw Mill and Lime Quarry as a laborer. In September 1890, the regiment was reorganized and twenty-five men from Company M were merged into Company B, including Roshier. The remaining men in Company M went to Company H. Along with this change, 2nd Lt. John Alexander was transferred to Fort Robinson and replaced by the only other African American army officer, 2nd Lt. Charles Young. A graduate of West Point, Charles Young had roomed with John Alexander at the military academy. It is noteworthy that the only two black officers in the U.S. Army were carefully placed in command of only black enlisted men. Company B remained at Fort Duchesne during the rest of the year, however soldiers in the Ninth Cavalry, Company D were under orders to quell the uprising of the Sioux at Pine Ridge Agency during the winter of 1890 and into 1891—one of the last engagements with hostile forces for the Buffalo Soldiers.

In March 1891, the men in Company B were ordered to remove drifting snow on the Nine Mile Road from the newly established Smith Ranch all the way to Whitmore Park.[33] a distance of 45 miles. "Pairs of horses on a team would have to be shuttled from the rear forward as one pair after another exhausted themselves beating the crusted snow, pawing it to break passage."[41]

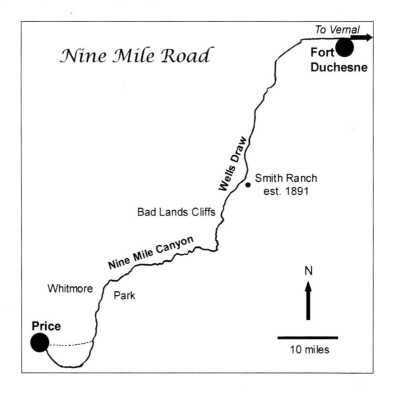

Nine Mile Road, constructed in 1886–1887 by soldiers of the Ninth Cavalry, was critical to the functioning of Fort Duchesne because it provided access to the railway and telegraph lines located in Price, established in that community in 1883. The soldiers built a road through rough and steeply rocky landscape at elevations up to 7,400 feet, initially following an old Indian trail. The resultant road opened up new country and played an important role in the growth of the Uinta Basin. A one-way, roughly 85-mile trip from Fort Duchesne to Price took three hard, long days of travel by horseback. A roundtrip wagon ride took a week. Over this road stagecoaches carried passengers and mail, freighters drove teams of horses hauling goods, and ranchers herded cattle. The road has been proclaimed "the greatest contribution the army made in the Uinta Basin."[40]

Entering his fourth year of military service, Roshier performed duties as he was told: drill, march, patrol, labor at Saw Mill or Lime Quarry, fetch horses and supplies from the railway depot at Price and maintain the road to the fort. These duties were not hazardous or particularly exhausting. Nonetheless, in June of 1891 Roshier fell ill. Illness was uncommon yet persistent among the troops. On average, between six and twelve enlisted men per month in the Ninth Cavalry were reported being "sick in post hospital" during Roshier's time in the military. From two to four cases of death from disease per year were reported during 1888–1890, the causes of which were listed as pneumonia, consumption and one death from "acute phthisis rheumatism."[33] Roshier was transported by train to the new U.S. Army and Navy General Hospital at Hot Springs, Arkansas where he became a patient.

The thirty-bed military hospital was established in 1887 with the rationale that the mineral waters of the hot springs would be therapeutic for injured, sick and disabled soldiers. Roshier remained at the hospital under medical treatment for five months, from June through October 1891.[33] At the young age of twenty-five, Roshier was confined to a sick-bed with "rheumatism and disease of the heart." Rheumatic fever was the third most common cause of troop impairment during and after the Civil War. "Rheumatism" was an old term applied to symptoms including painful and swollen joints, rash, elevated pulse and pain in the heart region, probably from pericarditis. The illness could result in death, so doctors confined their patients to rest until all symptoms abated. The only treatment of the time was the administration of colchicum, made from the autumn crocus flower.[42]

Having recovered sufficiently to be released from the hospital, Roshier was transferred to Fort Omaha, Nebraska where he was discharged on December 10, 1891. His action papers read, "For Disability, Roshier H. Creecy, Private, Company B, Dec. 10. 1891, Fort Omaha, Neb. F. S. Sergeant gives character Excellent."[33]

Roshier filed for his pension of $12 per month, to commence on January 15, 1892, in Washington, D.C.[43] The pension was awarded for "rheumatism and disease of the heart."[43] Roshier was either fortunate or shrewd to finagle a disability at discharge, because at that time Congress only granted pensions for veterans who became disabled while on active duty. Indian Wars veterans were not granted a service pension until 1917, and even then, eligibility depended on whether the service member's company had participated in specified campaigns. For example, Buffalo Soldiers in

Company D were granted pensions for their role in the Ute War of 1879, however, none of the Buffalo Soldiers who served in the New Mexico Territory from 1876–1881 had status as "Indian War Campaigners." It was not until 1927 that Congress passed an act to provide pensions for all veterans, regardless of military activity.[44]

Roshier's pension award from the U.S. Army[21]

In his later years, Roshier freely embellished the account surrounding his pension award. He made no mention of lying sick in a hospital bed for five months. Rather, he wove an exciting and funny story about being under attack, diving under a table to dodge a fusillade of shots only to find that one of his commanding officers had already hidden himself under the table! Roshier confided to his listeners that he made a deal with his commanding office not to tell anyone he found him hiding if, in exchange, the C.O. would promise to make sure Roshier received a pension at discharge. It suited Roshier to cast himself as a blackmailer rather than as an invalid.

Chapter 3

Washington, D.C.

Roshier returned to Washington, D.C. in early 1892. He was now twenty-six years old. Washington was rapidly growing with an influx of immigrants and African Americans drawn to its more tolerant social atmosphere. In 1890, the city had a population of about 230,400 and by 1900 the population had grown 21 percent to 278,700 people, with the largest percentage of African Americans of any city in the nation.[45] Motorized street-cars carried commuters of all races along the major thoroughfares. While some institutions were segregated, the city had fewer Jim Crow laws than most and there were hundreds of African American-owned businesses.[45] The heart of the city was Pennsylvania Avenue along which were beautiful parks, opera houses, banks and hotels, within sight of saloons and "bawdy houses" where liquor and vice flowed freely, if you were looking for it. Roshier felt comfortable returning to this city and was open to its possibilities.

In September 1892, Roshier crowded with other citizens along Pennsylvania Avenue to watch the parade of the Grand Army of the Republic, soldiers of the Civil War who held annual "encampments" to honor Civil War veterans. This event was transformed into Armistice Day following World War I, and later denoted as Veterans Day in the mid-1950s. *The New York Times* described the decorations, reporting that the State, War, and Navy Department buildings were "almost completely covered with flags and streamers," while the Post Office Department building was festooned with "portraits, in heroic size" of President Lincoln and Generals Grant, Sherman and Sheridan. The decorations on the White House and Treasury were "elaborate."[46]

Parade of the Grand Army of the Republic, Pennsylvania Avenue, Washington, D.C., September 1892[47]

Roshier met a beautiful young woman named Adeline Savannah Georgia "Georgie" Arnold. Georgie was born in May 1876 in Virginia to Jane Arnold, an African American woman born in about 1844. It is believed that Georgie's father was named Gustav G. Offterdinger, born in Baden-Württemberg, Germany in 1836.[48, 49] Gustav immigrated to America in 1853 and started a butcher shop in Lynchburg,

Virginia. To supply meat for his shop, Gustav operated small cattle feed-lots, including one in Brookland, a neighborhood in the northeast quadrant of Washington, D.C.[50] Like many southern white men of his era, Gustav had two families—one white and one black. Gustav married Adeline Wachter, an immigrant from Switzerland, and they had four children. Adeline died in 1872. Gustav developed a relationship with Jane Arnold. In the 1880 U.S. Federal Census, Jane Arnold lived with her children on Twelfth Street NW, Washington D.C. where she and her eldest daughter, Fannie, worked as servants. The two youngest children, Albert and Georgie, completed the household.

On September 27, 1893, Roshier H. Creecy, twenty-seven, married Georgie Arnold, seventeen, in Washington, D.C. They were married by Pastor Walter H. Brooks in the Nineteenth Street Baptist Church, first organized in 1839 as the First Colored Baptist Church of Washington. Georgie's older sister, Fannie E. Arnold, a man named Robert E. Lee, and the pastor's wife, Mrs. Brooks, served as witnesses.[51]

Roshier's affiliation with this historic church strengthened his resolve to reject mistreatment based on race. Pastor Brooks held a formidable reputation as an advocate for racial equality. During Pastor Brooks' tenure, the church hosted the first meeting of the National Federation of Afro-American Women and events for African American Civil War veterans.[46]

On November 21, 1896, their son, Nathan "Crusy" was born in Brookland.[52] Roshier had a beautiful wife, an infant son and a steady income from his pension. Despite his blessings, Roshier became restless. He was not the kind of man to dwell in contentment. His time in the Army and Navy

Hospital had given Roshier plenty of time to think: his life could be cut short, and he wanted to feel the excitement of new adventures, of new challenges.

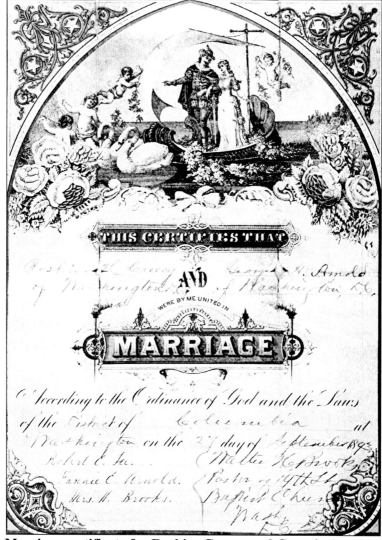

Marriage certificate for Roshier Creecy and Georgie Arnold, September 27, 1893[21]

Additionally, Roshier chafed at the endemic racism he encountered in the city. While Washington D.C. had relatively few laws mandating racial segregation, a man of color still suffered indignities of daily life in a white-dominated culture.[45]

In the summer of 1897, Roshier, along with thousands of other astounded hopefuls, read in the city's newspapers, such as *The National Tribune*, about a tremendous gold discovery in the Klondike, Yukon Territory, Canada. Creeks containing large gold nuggets were discovered in the fall of

Georgie Creecy, Washington, D.C., 1894[21]

1896, but the oncoming winter prevented traffic from the Klondike to the outside world. It was not until June 1897 that the first steamers carrying the newly mined gold arrived on the West Coast and word rapidly spread.

Newspapers at the time reported that the two steamers departing from Saint Michael, Alaska, the *Excelsior* (which docked in San Francisco) and the *Portland* (which arrived in Seattle), had discharged hordes of gold miners carrying sacks of gold totaling $1,139,000 worth of gold. The gold miners had come from Dawson, a city located in the Klondike. Journalists around the world publicized the discovery, encouraging a stampede of prospectors over the next few years who dreamed of becoming wealthy.[53, 54]

Like many others, Roshier was continuing to suffer from the consequences of the Panic of 1896, an acute economic depression that precipitated bank failures, unemployment and uncertainty. The large gold fields of the Klondike enticed men with possibilities of a shorter path to financial security. What of the possible perils and suffering if one could amass a fortune through hard labor, independence? As he mulled over the daily reports in the newspapers promoting travel and promising adventure laced with riches, Roshier recalled the Gilsonite miners of the Uinta and their money that flowed through the saloons and boarding-houses of the Duchesne Strip. He realized that riches were not only to be found in prospecting for gold, but also in separating gold from its miner through a business venture, such as operating a roadhouse. At the age of thirty-one, Roshier resolved to join the stampede to the Klondike. He was determined to become a success and make his fortune! Perhaps unconsciously, his steps led him to seek the freedom to shape his life unencumbered by expectations of family and limitations from society. Roshier left Georgie and their one-year-old son, Nathan, in the fall of 1897, traveling by train to Seattle, Washington, where he found a place to stay. From there, Roshier planned the next leg of his journey north. He never returned home.

Chapter 4

Journey to the Klondike

The various routes to the Klondike gold fields, as promoted in the news and by commercial operators, harbored untruths and uncertainties. Tabloid stories about the Klondike spread misinformation and exaggeration, resulting in legions of men becoming dangerously ill-equipped, broke or disillusioned along their journey north during the summer of 1897. Roshier's challenge was to separate truth from fiction in selecting the best route and in making his preparations. There were two possible ways to reach the Klondike from Seattle: the expensive but faster all-water route, or the more arduous but supposedly cheaper water-land route. The all-water 4,700 mile journey meant he would have to buy passage on a steamer from Seattle across the northern Pacific Ocean to Saint Michael Island, located off the Alaskan coast near the Yukon River delta. From Saint Michael he would need to pay passage on a riverboat to travel up the Yukon River to Dawson. The price for a ticket on the all-water route during the last half of 1897 was $1,000.[55] He didn't have that kind of money! In addition, the Yukon River would be freezing up soon, closing off the all-water route for the next eight months. Roshier decided to take the water-land route, accessed by taking a steamer to Juneau, Alaska, and from there boarding a smaller steamer to the ports of either Dyea or Skagway. From

Dyea, one followed the 33-mile-long Chilkoot Pass Trail over a 3,057-foot summit to Lake Lindeman. From Skagway, one followed the 44-mile-long White Pass Trail over a 2,865-foot summit to Lake Bennett. Both trails converged at a tent city called Bennett Camp at the head of Lake Bennett, headwaters of the Yukon River which flowed past Dawson, gateway to the Klondike gold fields.[55] From his time in the army, Roshier had a taste of the hardship of frontier travel, but he had never experienced the extreme cold of the frozen north.

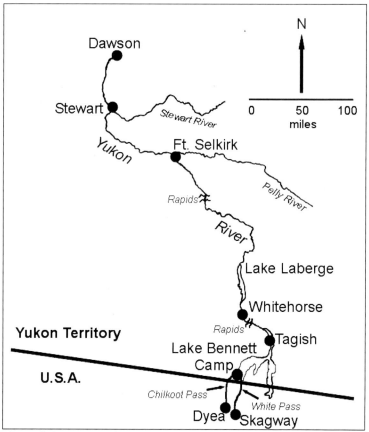

Map of the routes from Dyea and Skagway to Lake Bennett, headwaters of the Yukon River, which flows to Dawson

Roshier considered the thousands of men who had already embarked on the journey to cross the Chilkoot and White Passes during late summer and early fall of 1897; their tales of hardship and horror were drifting into Seattle. The British Yukon Company had supposedly constructed a pack trail through the White Pass summit, preliminary to surveys for a future railway, but those who attempted this route found boulders and sharp rocks covered in wet, slippery moss. Over this impossible terrain pack-horses slipped and fell down the steep mountain sides, thousands of them, to their deaths. By late summer in 1897, the White Pass Trail became so bad that the miners themselves closed it off, until an alternative trail could be constructed of logs over the gullies and boulders. As winter advanced and the muddy trail froze, the miners allowed the White Pass Trail to reopen. The Chilkoot Pass Trail was little better, with scaling the last 2 miles to the summit like alpine rock climbing, the hardest physical exertion of the trip. The stampeders had to portage their outfits in stages, toiling for weeks, sometimes months, back and forth, caching bundles of supplies under rocks or high in trees so animals or thieves would not find them. To ease their suffering, those with money hired local native Tlingit men to pack their outfits over the summits at 12–20 cents a pound.[55, 56] Roshier decided he would travel to the closest port, Skagway, and from there portage his goods up the White Pass Trail, which was longer than the Chilkoot Pass Trail, but not as steep.

Winter weather settled over the trails. The Canadian government and newspapers cautioned men not to embark for the Klondike in winter because "suffering will be great."[56] Despite this warning, the tide of men continued to surge north. They boarded steamers with sled dogs and pack horses as the new strategy was to pull their supplies on sleds over the snow and ice, either by hand or by dogs or horses. Gliding supplies on sled runners was much easier than packing supplies through mud on your back. While the snow made travel easier, the arctic cold made travel more dangerous.

Fearful that with winter approaching, the onslaught of stampeders into the Klondike region would consume limited food, the Canadian government mandated that each person entering Canada bring a one-year supply of food to avert starvation. The Yukon River, the means by which supplies historically entered the Klondike, is frozen until June, so all goods had to arrive during the open-water period or people were out of luck. The mandate was enforced by the North-West Mounted Police who established customs posts at Chilkoot and White Pass summits.[56] A one-year supply of food plus all the equipment for the journey to Dawson weighed a ton!

Roshier was shocked to learn that the cost of a "grubstake" to the Klondike was at a minimum $1,000— at Seattle prices! The cost would steeply escalate if he tried to purchase items along the way or in Dawson.

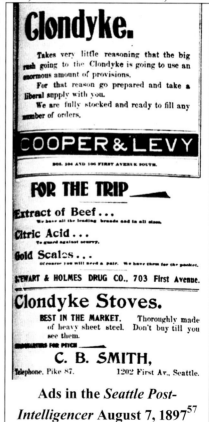

Ads in the *Seattle Post-Intelligencer* August 7, 1897[57]

He made a list of needed items, gleaned from advertisements in newspapers and word on the street. Seattle was overrun with would-be prospectors, and stores vied keenly for their business. In addition to food, Roshier needed an outfit of heavy clothes (preferably fur garments) and boots for winter, as well as lighter clothes for summer; a camp outfit, including wool blankets, a canvas tent, rope, frying pan, coffee pot, plate and cup, a small sheet-iron stove with lengths of pipe, candles, matches, wash-basin, soap, various medicines, a shaving kit and snow glasses; a building outfit, including a hammer, assorted nails, saws, ax, caulking iron, pitch and oakum; a mining outfit, including a pick, shovel, gold pan and gold dust bags; to provide fresh meat he'd need a Winchester rifle, one hundred bullets, a knife, fishing line and hooks; and oil-skin bags to keep provisions dry. A sampling of suggested Klondike supplies for one man for a year follows:[55]

Flour	500 lbs	Stout pants or jeans	2 pr
Corn-meal	100 lbs	Jacket	1
Oats	50 lbs	Heavy wool socks	3 pr
Beans	150 lbs	Ordinary socks	3 pr
Coffee	25 lbs	Lined leather mittens	2 pr
Tea	12 lbs	Rubber boots	2 pr
Salt	10 lbs	Shoes, stout and heavy	2 pr
Sugar	75 lbs	Mosquito netting	5 yds
Dried fruit	100 lbs	Heavy long underwear	3 suits
Bacon	150 lbs	Towels	2
Dried potatoes	40 lbs	Citric acid (for scurvy)	1 lb

Although Roshier preferred being alone, he realized that teaming up with other men would reduce the cost of camping and building equipment by distributing purchase of the needed items among them, and spread out the weight and labor in portaging supplies up the steep pass into Canada. Roshier found three traveling companions named E. B. Davies, C. G. Fowler and G. McQueeni.[58] After boarding a steamer in Seattle, they traveled up the Inside Passage to Juneau and from there to the head of the Lynn Canal.

During a steady snow in January of 1898, Roshier's steamer idled into the port of Skagway.[59] Skagway was a newly formed city of approximately a hundred white tents and rough frame buildings housing seven thousand men and several enterprising women. The surrounding snow-capped mountains and ice fields of the Alaska Boundary Range loomed over the thin shoreline. Freight and passengers were disgorged from the steamer in utter confusion. Landing the freight was up to the passengers; the steamship people refused to assume responsibility. A jumbled mess of boxes and people began to pile up on the wharf and spill onto the beach.[56]

Unbeknownst to the new arrivals, outlaws had stationed lookouts at the wharf where they selected newcomers for victimization. Roshier had stepped into Soapy Smith's territory. "Soapy" was an alias for Jefferson Randolph Smith, a crime boss who had organized a cadre of thugs,

Soapy Smith[60]

card sharks, cut-throats and highwaymen in Skagway and Dyea to commit fraud, theft and murder. Soapy's headquarters was his saloon in Skagway, "Jeff Smith's

Parlor." Soapy had traveled from his successful criminal enterprises in Colorado to Alaska in the summer of 1897 when he heard about the Klondike gold strike, planning to swindle and rob unsuspecting prospectors on their way to the gold fields. His men and women plagued unwary prospectors in the towns of Dyea and Skagway and along the trails. On the American side of the border, there was virtually no presence of the law, and the lone U. S. marshal for the region was soon on Soapy's payroll. Their prey were defrauded in town using a phony telegraph office; their pockets were picked clean in the bars; they were cheated at gambling; men were robbed of their outfits and money along the trails before they could reach the protection of the North-West Mounted Police at the Canadian border. Soapy was finally shot dead in the street in Skagway on July 4, 1898, ending the reign of his criminal gang.[61]

Idle men in front of "Jeff Smith's Parlor," Soapy Smith's criminal headquarters in Skagway, 1898[62]

Roshier and his companions found a scrap of frozen ground to erect a canvas tent and set about organizing their supplies. They would camp here for awhile, exploring Skagway for news about the trail. During the next few days they watched as groups of men stole away from the tent city in the direction of the trail-head, a steady stream of men, dogs, sleds, horses and heavy packs. "The crowd pouring over the White Pass was such as the world had never seen before."[56] Men would go up laden and come back down empty, back and forth in a relay. They watched, too, as discouraged and weary men came down from the trail for good. The tidbits of news and sometimes conflicting advice that Roshier heard in Skagway went something like this: wait to climb the trail until March or April, after the deep cold is past, yet when there is still snow for sledding supplies; don't travel over the pass during March and April, when avalanches can come down and wipe you off the trail; pilfering has been going on so keep your rifle within easy reach; it'll take you thirty round trips, over three months, to ferry your supplies to Lake Bennett; at the border, you need extra money to pay the constables a

Winter trail up the White Pass, March 29, 1899[63]

40

customs tax on American goods being packed into Canada—25 percent of the cost of your outfit![55, 56] Brooding by the campfire, Roshier realized that the trip was going to take longer and cost more than he had anticipated.

After dividing their outfits into small bundles, Roshier and his companions began the tedious process of ferrying their load over the White Pass Trail in stages. They had constructed a hand sled that three of them took turns hauling. The fourth man remained in camp to guard their remaining gear. At the end of the day, the travelers made camp, and two hiked back down the trail empty handed to their initial site, leaving the fourth man to guard the advancing pile. In this way they moved their load from one camp site to another slowly up the trail. For the first 5 miles, the trail was broad and climbed gently through a forest of

Men pull sleds up the steep winter trail, December 1897[47]

large cottonwood, hemlock and spruce trees. The trail progressed into alpine tundra, where firewood became scarce and the temperatures dipped to −50°F on windswept mountain ridges. Branches of dwarf willow were stripped for whatever warmth they could provide in the small camp stoves. The trail narrowed to 2 feet in some places with a sheer cliff on one side and a steep drop-off on the other. The slippery boulders and sharp rocks that had hindered summer travelers were covered by up to 200 inches of snow, but ice sheets imposed treacherous footing on steep terrain, with men and pack animals

41

struggling to gain ground. The cold numbed their fingers and toes and frosted their exposed faces. Snow storms delayed travel for days as men huddled together inside their canvas tents, lines straining to hold the flapping sides. Discarded items littered the trail as men lightened their loads to hasten their departure from the frigid mountains. As the days got longer with approaching spring, sunlight on the snow was glaring, and tinted-glass goggles were needed to prevent snow blindness. It took three months to get their outfits over the trail, with Roshier and his companions likely hiking 1,000 miles or more.[53, 55, 56]

As Roshier trudged out of the mountains, the trail dropped into a valley with air so warm he was stunned by the rapid transition in temperature. Only a few snow patches lingered amid the brown grasses and brush of the valley floor. They arrived at Lake Bennett in May of 1898. Here, thousands of stampeders, resting from the travails of their winter journeys through the White and Chilkoot Passes, had formed a bustling city of hundreds of tents. Most were waiting for the lake ice to thaw (which usually occurred in late May or early June) so they could launch their boats, scows or rafts into the chain of lakes that formed the headwaters of the Yukon River. Along the lake's shore, boat-building was occurring at a feverish pace. A ready supply of timber surrounding the lake supplied lumber. The noise of whip saws and hammers was constant. Watercraft of every design, shape and size were in various stages of development. Several enterprising groups had decided to make their fortune not in prospecting for gold, but in providing well-built boats to would-be miners for $75 each. Other entrepreneurs had set up tents housing hot baths, barber-shops, restaurants and saloons.[55]

Tent city at Lake Bennett, where Klondike stampeders waited for the ice to go out, May 1898[53]

Roshier and his companions made camp, then threaded their way through the tent-city vendors, eagerly taking advantage of a hot bath and cold liquor. They would remain at Lake Bennett a month while they built a scow and waited for break-up. In spring of 1898, the favorite vessel being crafted at Lake Bennett was a scow, about 25 feet long, drawing two feet of water or more when loaded.[55] To make a scow, trees (mostly spruce) were felled, cut into logs, and dragged to a building site. The logs were whipsawed into boards. To whipsaw, one man stood on top of the log to guide the saw and lift it for the next cut, while a second man stood at the bottom to pull it through the log along a chalk mark. There were occasional arguments as to who was doing the most work! The boards, usually about 10 inches wide and an inch thick, were rough-planed square and lashed or nailed in layers

43

to form sides that flared up, a beam 6 or 7 feet wide and a stern "wide and square"[56] With close to a ton of supplies per person, and the weight of four men on board, the scow would sit heavy in the water. The oakum and pitch that they had carried over the White Pass was unpacked and used to caulk the seams of the floorboards and sides of the scow to make it waterproof. The green lumber would shrink, making the scow leak like a sieve, so the oakum and pitch were frequently reapplied. In addition to sail canvas attached to a mast, the scow was rigged with oars. The men took time to make the scow sound, knowing it must withstand rough conditions and last the 550-mile-long trip to Dawson.[55, 56, 64]

Lake Bennett sits at the head of a series of interconnected lakes. Just a day's journey across Lake Bennett is Tagish Lake, and it was here that the North-West Mounted Police established a Canadian Customs Office. A newly built log barracks housed ten to twelve constables, affectionately known as "Mounties," who carried out various official duties. One duty was to collect a customs tax on American goods being brought into Canada. Duty was assessed at 30–35 percent of the stated value of hardware, 15–20 percent of the stated value of provisions and tobacco was taxed at 50 cents a pound. On average, a man's entire outfit could be taxed at 25 percent of its value—steep![55] When prospectors came up short of the cash demanded, the customs inspector could, in lieu of money, collect fees in the form of labor, usually whipsawing lumber. Or the inspector would allow goods to be held in trust until payment could be sent. The Mounties also issued a miner's license for $10, which gave a man the right to seek gold in the Yukon region for one year.

The Mounties instituted strict regulations regarding boats and pilots following the 1897 gold rush stampede, when unsuitable water craft were launched into the Yukon River and capsized in the rapids. The Mounties got fed up with fishing several hundred drowned victims out of the river. When stampeders arrived at Lake Bennett in 1898, the Mounties inspected each boat for adequacy and assessed the competency of the pilot—if found lacking, they required the boat be piloted by a commercial captain. In typical efficient fashion, the Mounties assigned a number to each water craft, levied a boat registration fee, and recorded the name and place of origin of each person on the boat. Women and children were forbidden to travel through the rapids—they had to hike around.[53, 55, 56]

A scow with two sails and five passengers, plus their outfits, at Lake Bennett in 1897[47]

By the time the lake ice melted in spring of 1898, the Mounties had inspected and assigned numbers to 7,124 boats embarking on the Yukon River from Lake Bennett to Dawson City, averaging five people per boat.[53, 56] On June 6, a constable approached Roshier and his companions asking for their names, which he hurriedly wrote in his ledger, scripting the first initials and surname of each person. The names were phonetically spelled, according to what he heard the person impatiently bark out. The constable assigned no. 2102 to Roshier's scow, and wrote the following names, all from Seattle, Washington: "E. B. Davies, C. G. Fowler, R. Crezy and G. McQueeni."[58]

Portion of a ledger of names, place of origin and boat number assigned by the North-West Mounted Police to stampeders at Lake Bennett in 1898[58]

With the scow resting in the water and their load lashed tight, Roshier poled the craft into deeper water and hoisted the sail. They were off! The wind created small chop on the lake as they sailed down the right side, angling for a sluggish 2 mile-long stream emptying into Tagish Lake. In Tagish Lake, they found hundreds of ducks bobbing in a cove, evidence of the spring migration. They sailed for about 18 miles, looking for an outlet on the left side, a 6-mile-long river emerging into Lake Marsh. This lake is 25 miles long and empties into the upper Yukon River, also called Lewes River. Roshier let out a troll line; after an hour, he was rewarded with a tug from a fine large trout which they kept for dinner. At the far end of Lake Marsh they rowed to shore, secured the scow, and made camp for the night. A few dozen other boats, scows and rafts had also pulled ashore. A good rest was needed for the next day because they would encounter the first of the rapids 20 miles downriver in Miles Canyon.[55, 56]

Klondikers in scows sailing down Lake Marsh, June 1898[65]

Miles Canyon is 100 feet wide, lined with perpendicular basalt rock walls that foment the river into a seething churn, at the bottom of which is a powerful eddy. As the small flotilla from Lake Marsh drew near the rapids, pilots rowed to shore so they could assess the rapids for danger. Watching the pitching and heaving troughs of water in the canyon, not many wanted to risk the loss of their outfits, or their lives, in the rapids.

A scow navigates Miles Canyon, 1897[47]

Roshier's group decided to break down their load and portage around, pulling the scow over log rollers. It took the rest of the day to portage around the rapids. The next morning, they floated downriver for only 2 miles before another set of rapids, the Whitehorse Rapids, impeded progress. Again, the flotilla pulled ashore to weigh the risk of plowing through. At these rapids, enterprising commercial river captains offered to pilot any boat through the rapids for \$10–\$20 per boat.[55, 66] Roshier and his companions again opted to portage. The following day, they floated 28 miles to the head of Lake Laberge where they made camp.[55, 56]

Before the Yukon River reaches the town of Whitehorse, it widens into Lake Laberge. This 30 mile-long expanse of river is cold and late to lose its cover of spring ice. Its waters are often buffeted by winds, so it was no surprise to find the lake alive in whitecaps. The next day, the scow scudded along with wind in its sail. Near the lake's outlet, large pans of ice were still present. The men poled through the pans to reach shore for the night's camp. A roaring fire was built, the skillet unpacked and bacon tossed in to fry. Additional fare was flapjacks and rolled oat mush with condensed milk and sugar. After months of hardship on the journey north, Roshier relaxed. As he gazed at the majestic expanse of wilderness around him, he heard loons call and watched a beaver create soundless wakes in the nearshore waters. Mosquitoes came out as the winds died down, and the men sought relief from their bites by tossing green wood on the fire to create more smoke. In June, the sky in northern latitudes does not get dark because the earth's northern pole is tilted toward the sun. Evening twilight persists into morning daybreak. Roshier felt at ease in this place, with these people, where judgment of a man was based on his grit and character, not on his race. He did not feel confined by Jim Crow in the Yukon, and this freedom contributed to his peacefulness that night.

There was no wind in the morning. They pushed aside pans of ice and aimed for the lake's outlet. Rocks poked up in the swift current downstream of Lake Laberge, and with luck, they successfully maneuvered around these sharp obstacles. They floated 30 miles to the confluence of the Hootalinqua River; from there, it was another 135 miles until the next set of rapids, called Five Finger Rapids. The men floated and camped their way down river. White birch trees were seen for the first time, and large cottonwoods began to replace spruce as the river dropped in elevation. Occasionally, they saw small encampments of Athabascan native people at the river's edge and knew if they pulled ashore, the natives would offer to sell fur mittens, caps, skins and game meat. When they reached Five Finger Rapids, they saw five reddish rocks of large size standing in a row across the river. They were advised by fellow travelers to keep to the right and they would be all right. Six miles downriver was a little set of rapids on the western shore, called the Rink Rapids. Thereafter, the river offered smooth sailing for 230 miles to Dawson—at least that was the rumor. In actuality, the river widened out forming channels and small wooded islands. Sometimes they followed the wrong channel into shallow water where the scow became grounded; it was a big pain to heft the scow out into faster and deeper current. When they got to the confluence of Stewart River, active with a line of tents, cabins, and people, they knew they were close. Many boats had hauled out at Stewart River, with men intending to spend the summer prospecting for gold in its tributaries. "Keep to the right and look sharp or you'll be carried past Dawson," was the advice they were given the next morning as they cast off.[55, 56]

Chapter 5

Dawson

Three weeks after pushing off from Lake Bennett, Roshier and his companions rowed to shore at Dawson. Dawson sits on the east bank of the Yukon River below the mouth of the Klondike River. A suburb of Dawson, called Klondike City, or "Lousetown"[56] sprawled on the east bank above the Klondike River. The Yukon River here is about a half-mile wide and flows fairly swiftly. Dawson is built on muskeg, which is swampy in summer but hard and dry in winter. In 1898, there were about three hundred cabins and other buildings, including a police barracks of thirty Mounties. A ragged variety of twenty-eight hundred white canvas tents stretched up the hillside. The only street, Main Street, was lined by two-story log hotels and restaurants as well as saloons, dance halls, gaming halls, an opera house, mining-broker's offices and a bakery. There were two large stores in Dawson, the Alaska Commercial Company and Northern American Transportation and Trading Company. Dawson also boasted several newspapers, banks, barbershops, blacksmiths, laundries, churches and Saint Mary's Hospital, where patients were treated for typhoid and dysentery during summer and scurvy and rheumatism during winter. On the outskirts of town were several saw-mills. The population of Dawson had grown from about 500 people in the winter of 1896 to 4,000 people in 1897 and to 20,000 people in 1898. It reached its peak population of 40,000 in 1899. A journalist proclaimed the population of Dawson to be "A motley gathering from every walk of life and corner of the country."[56]

There was a carnival atmosphere with an international flavor: while most people were white male Americans, there were some African Americans, Canadians, Australians, Englishmen, Japanese, and a few women. The Klondike leveled class and race distinctions because all who reached Dawson had required the same tough spirit and had earned their freedom from the norms of society.[64] While the city hummed with hope, only about 3 percent of those who came to Dawson to strike it rich actually made any money.[53, 56, 61]

Klondike City in the foreground, with Dawson sitting across the Klondike River as it enters the Yukon River, 1899[53]

It was a good thing that Main Street was lined with a board sidewalk, because when Roshier and his companions arrived in July, the streets were muddy; in some places the mud was knee-deep! In the constant daylight of summer, Dawson was lively, open twenty-four hours a day with much "carousing and drunkenness." The Mounties kept it under control, however, by banning pistols in town and relegating most of the prostitution to Klondike City. On Sundays, gambling and the sale of liquor were outlawed.[61] Merchandise was offloaded around the clock from steamers that arrived from downriver, bringing supplies and mail from Alaska and the West Coast of the United States. By September 1, 1898, fifty-six steamboats had delivered 7,500 tons of supplies to Dawson.[56]

Main Street in Dawson with a horse-drawn wagon stuck in the mud, summer 1898[53]

In Roshier's early days of exploring Dawson, someone pointed out George Carmack, the man who had started the Klondike Gold Rush. The story was repeated endlessly in saloons.

In 1896, an American named Joe Ladue, who had come to the Yukon in 1882 to trade and prospect, came across Robert Henderson, another prospector. Joe suggested Robert look along the Klondike River for gold. Robert only found a little bit, about 8 cents per pan. Robert then came across **George Carmack** and his brothers-in-law, Skookum Jim and Tagish Charley, who were fishing in the Klondike River. Robert told them about

George Carmack, Dawson[47]

his mining there. When the three fishermen had caught enough fish for the day and were headed back to camp, they tried panning. They came up with $4 per pan—big nuggets and lots of them! They filed their claims of the big strike without telling Robert. There was some consternation that non-miners had made the biggest gold strike of the north.[53, 64]

Having reached their destination, Roshier and his companions drifted apart, each seeking their own destiny. The newcomers from Lake Bennett soon spread to the surrounding gold fields, looking for land that had not yet been claimed or for a job as a laborer at a developed mine, so they could earn wages for their own "stake."[61] Purchase of an existing gold mining claim during the height of the gold rush was out of reach for most, with the price of $1,000 a foot for good paying dirt—too much money for a "Chee Chacoe," the Athabascan name for "new men."[55] By July of 1898, over 30 miles of creeks were staked and close to ten thousand placer mining claims had been recorded in Dawson. As summer work began, "whole creeks were ripped and gutted. Nothing but flood and fire is so ruthless as a miner."[56]

Roshier hitched a ride on a wagon taking supplies to the gold fields located on the various creeks from 8 to 50 miles outside of town. Laborers earned wages from $15 to $20 a day and were paid in gold dust and nuggets. Additional currency was furs and dollars. Laborers could accumulate a respectable sack of gold through wages—if a man could forgo the expensive temptations found in Dawson. Still, a man had to be frugal if he wanted to save enough for a stake.

A miner pays his saloon tab in Dawson with gold dust, 1899[53]

Items were expensive in Dawson because of the cost of freight. The smallest price for any item in town was "two bits" or 50 cents. When supplies flowed into town steadily from the steamers, Roshier could expect to buy 50 pounds of flour for $6.25 or five skins (fox or marten). Sugar was 25 cents a pound, eggs were $1.50 per dozen, tea was $1 per pound, tobacco was $1.50 per pound, and a glass of liquor in the saloon was 50 cents. A meal in a restaurant cost $1.50. But at the end of winter, when supplies ran low, prices doubled.[55] The stores and saloons had a gold scale at the end of their counters because prices were paid in gold dust. Gold was exchanged for paper money at the rate of $16 per troy ounce.

In the gold fields, Roshier saw four levels of mining aimed at finding gold on a stream bottom or in a "bench" of an old river channel—panning, rocking, sluicing and dredging. Panning is the smallest level, where a prospector "tries" creeks by digging out dirt and sloshing it around in a pan with water. Since gold is heavy, it sinks to the bottom of the pan and the lighter dirt is washed away with every swirl of the pan. A final swish of water carefully separates gold flecks from the remaining sand. The flakes are picked out, secured in a buckskin bag, and the panning process is repeated. Every miner carried a scale to weigh the "color," so he knew how much each pan produced. Five cents' worth of gold per pan was considered pay for summer work, 10 cents per pan was considered pay for winter work, while 25 cents per pan was considered rich. If it didn't look like an area would produce enough gold, the miner needed to prospect elsewhere.[55, 56]

On a larger level, rockers are used to accelerate the amount of dirt processed. A wooden rocker resembling a cradle is built, with a perforated top and a sloping bottom called an "apron." Dirt is shoveled onto the top, then water is poured in and the miner rocks the slush down. The gold ore

Panning, 1898[67]   **Rocker, 1898**[67]

falls through the perforated top and lodges on the apron, which
is scooped up and mixed with mercury or "quicksilver."
Mercury adheres to the ore creating an amalgam. When the
amalgam is heated, mercury vaporizes, leaving behind gold.[55]
Unfortunately, the miners didn't know about the toxic effects
of mercury, which produces neurological and environmental
damage. Mercury vapors are carried by wind, deposited in
water, and accumulate in fish and other animals, poisoning
predators (including humans). Mercury contamination of
stream sediments from gold mining operations persists for
years.

Bigger placer mining operations use sluice boxes to
find gold. Sluices require a lot of water, usually produced by
damming a creek and digging ditches to the area. A sluice is a
wooden box, measuring 12 feet long, 12 inches deep and 1
foot across, with one end tapered so multiple boxes can be
fitted in tandem to make a long funnel. Attached to the bottom
of the box are small wooden cross pieces that create a "riffle"
when dirt is washed down. The riffle catches the heavier gold

particles and holds them from being washed out of the tunnel with the rest of the mud slurry. The "riffle concentrate" is then panned to further refine the separation of gold from black iron sand.[55]

Sluice boxes at Bonanza Creek, 1899[67]

A fourth method of gold mining, dredging, did not begin in the Klondike gold fields until June of 1901, when a dredge was installed on Bonanza Creek. The dredge scoops up dirt at a rate of a ton every two to three minutes. Although Bonanza Creek had been heavily mined, the dredge processed so much dirt that a lot of gold was found, so the dredge was deemed a success. Thereafter, large mining corporations employing dredges began to infiltrate the Klondike.[68] The old way of pick and shovel was being replaced by machinery.

Dredge at Bear Creek, 1913[67]

Roshier built a single-room log cabin near a rich-producing mine, joining scores of other miners doing the same thing. Most miners built cabins that measured 10' x 12', with logs 8" to 9" thick, stacked nine or ten high. Cracks between logs were chinked with moss. The roof was made of small poles, covered in moss, then in dirt, which sprouted grass over time. Windows were holes sawed in the sides with a white flour sack nailed over the opening as a cover. The floor was often dirt. A stove was placed in the middle of the cabin with its stove-pipe passing through a square oil can in the roof. A table, a stool and a bunk covered in spruce boughs lain over with skins and blankets, served as furnishings. Light was provided by candles or a kerosene lantern. In the evening, when his chores of splitting wood, hauling water and cooking were done, Roshier read books, magazines or old newspapers. He learned a trick of the far north: keep a vial of liquid mercury as a thermometer, because when it freezes (reaches its solid state) you know it is –40°F and to stay indoors.[55, 56]

Roshier intended to try his luck in the gold fields through the winter of 1898–1899. New finds occurred on a regular basis. Local newspapers often proclaimed the excitement of a new find in a creek somewhere, which would start a local stampede to that creek, "leading to either disgust or euphoria."[55] Black and white miners alike enjoyed the equal promise of opportunity in the Klondike. Yet Dawson society could sting Roshier with disrespectful racial slurs so common at the time as to be uttered with little thought, as evidenced in newspapers.

For social life, miners went to the saloons in Dawson to have fun. Dance-hall girls would waltz with anyone, and at the end of a short number, guide their partners to the bar for a glass of whiskey. The miner pulled out his gold poke, the bartender weighed out the bill in gold dust on a scale, returning the poke to the miner. This routine was repeated all night until the poke was deflated or the miner was smashed. While many miners were enticed to drink and gamble their hard-won gold dust, there were others who came to the Klondike looking to make a "home stake" —money to take back home.[55, 56]

As summer waned, the mining community of Dawson prepared for winter mining. Winter work was called drift mining or "drifting." Miners began by picking off a "muck" layer of mud and moss. In the early days, they built a wood fire to thaw the frozen ground. The rule was six hours of burning to thaw 6 inches of ground. Operations progressed to using steam heated in a boiler to thaw the ground. Steam was passed from the boiler through a rubber hose, at the end of which was a steel tube about 4 feet in length, which was driven into the frozen gravel. Steam was forced into the ground for a period of six to twelve hours. Thawing and digging were repeated. Shafts were dug vertically to bedrock, anywhere from 3 to 20 feet below the surface. Miners looked for the "pay streak" of gold in the layers down to bedrock. When a pay streak was found, they tunneled horizontally or "drifted" to follow the gold. Timbering to shore up the underground tunnels was seldom required because the frozen ground above formed "an extremely tenacious roof." [64] The dirt and gravel were hauled out of the tunnels using a windlass and piled on the surface in "dumps." The process of thawing ground, tunneling and hauling up dirt and gravel was repeated all winter. When the weather became warm enough to thaw the dump and creek, sluicing began. [68]

Creating gold-infused dumps in winter carried the risk of a spring flood or "freshet" washing the pile away before it could be processed, wasting a whole winter's work. In a 1902 report by the North-West Mounted Police commissioner on the Yukon Territory, the increasing incidence of spring floods in the gold fields was noted. Miners had cut all the timber near the creeks and with loss of shade, the snow cover melted rapidly causing freshets "doing considerable damage. . . Gold was lost during the spring freshets, when many of the dumps that had been brought to the surface during the winter were washed away." With rapid snow-melt and water runoff a drought ensued, leaving no water in the creek with which the miner could process his gold. "This is a real trouble the miner is afflicted with," wrote the commissioner.[70]

The left-over dirt and gravel from processed dumps was useful for road construction. Pack horses were used in summer to haul supplies in and gold out, while dog teams pulling sleds were used in winter. Because winter was the longest season of the year, dogs were essential to the miner for transportation and cost several hundred dollars each. In 1898, a journalist counted fifteen hundred dogs in Dawson.[56]

Surprisingly, with all the gold being transported from the gold fields, no great precautions were taken to guard against robbers. Upon reaching Dawson, miners had their gold assayed and received bank notes for the full value. The gold was packed into iron boxes and stored in the warehouses until the next steamer arrived. When banks came to town, gold was stored in bank vaults. Steamers took the gold down the Yukon River to Seattle and San Francisco. Each shipment of gold was accompanied by one policeman with a rifle.[56]

Roshier likely agreed with fellow American miners who considered Canadian mining laws and fees onerous. From the government's point of view, Americans were taking Canadian gold out of the country and the government meant to capture some of that wealth. From the American miner's point of view, "the government seems to do all it can to deter men [from prospecting], receiving half the ground and taxing them for their work . . . Because of the mining laws being so badly handled, people are scared to try mining."[61]

Laws governing gold mining in the Yukon Territory allowed one claim per person per creek (except the discoverer was allowed twice as much ground as the others), so it was important for the prospector to locate a claim on the best ground. A claim consisted of 500 feet along a creek, from bank to bank, up to 600 feet wide. A gold commissioner administered the mining laws and settled disputes. The law was enforced by the North-West Mounted Police, who also acted as magistrates. The government took a 10 percent tax of gold from a claim with an output of $500 a month or less, and 20 percent in tax for claims yielding greater than $500 a month.[55] Miners felt the 20 percent tax was imposed through "crass ignorance of the conditions of working and expense of mining, a tax likened to highway robbery."[61] A claim had a $15 annual registration fee and a $100 annual rental fee. In addition, every alternate claim in all placer grounds was to be reserved as the property of the government! Claims not worked for seventy-two hours were deemed abandoned, unless sickness or other cause, such as a leave of absence, was filed with the government. A leave of absence of a year was allowed if the miner showed that $1,000 had been spent on the claim without reasonable returns.[55, 61] The miners engaged in a covert protest by under-reporting their take.[64]

There is no record of Roshier having submitted an application for a gold mining claim in the Klondike.[71] However, the paperwork could have been lost. Years later, Roshier told a story about prospecting in the Klondike to his friend, Harry Leonard. While Roshier liked to spin tall tales, the following story could be true. "Before coming to the Koyukuk, Creecy had two claims on Hunker Creek. The claims had been previously worked, so there was no gold left, but Creecy had a plan. Every time someone came up the creek, he got busy panning. Remarkably, he always came up with a pan of gold in full sight of the newly arrived onlookers. Seeing the gold prompted a gullible prospector to buy his claims."[5]

In spring of 1899, news spread to people living in the creeks that a big fire had come "pretty near wiping out the town."[61] Being constructed of wood, and heating with flame, Dawson experienced several raging fires in its history, but rebuilding always began before the embers were cold. With the loss of a dwindling supply of provisions, people were overjoyed when the first steamer of the year arrived with fresh goods. "Miners waved their hats and cheered" when they saw the steamer, because the saloons had run out of whiskey![56]

That summer of 1899, gold was discovered in Nome and many left the Klondike for Alaska. A journalist wrote, "Nearly everybody is going to Nome."[61] The exodus marked the beginning of the end of the Klondike Gold Rush.

A line of 391 men leaving Dawson for Nome, September 1899[53]

The newspapers that had encouraged so many to stampede to Dawson lost interest in this story, highlighting instead the latest gold strikes elsewhere. Before the winter of 1899–1900 set in, many prospectors left Dawson to prospect in American territory, or head for home. "After the stampede to Nome, a cabin that had been selling for $500 could be had for the taking."[56]

It was hard getting mail in and out of Dawson. Perhaps these reasons compounded the lapse of communication between Roshier and Georgie. At least three months a year there was no mail because travel conditions were too dangerous – this was during freeze-up, when river ice jammed up, and during spring break-up, when rotting ice was treacherous.[61] Compounding the problems of transporting mail across vast distances of wilderness in often wicked weather, the Canadian government made the mistake of awarding the contract for carrying the Yukon mail to a man named Richardson, "who was a regular dummy."[61] No one was getting any mail! After much public outcry, the Mounties added the responsibility of carrying the Yukon mail from October 1897 to October 1898. The Mounties discovered 20 tons of mail scattered along the Yukon River between Dawson and Skagway. [61] Getting the mail to Dawson was not the end of the saga. There was no post office, just a tent, and only one government employee. People had to wait in line for days to get their mail. Further, there was no way to deliver the mail to those who were working their claims in the gold fields.[61]

As the months, then the years, dragged on in Roshier's absence, Georgie's family situation changed. Her older sister, Fannie, married Mark C. Thomas and moved to Pittsburgh, Pennsylvania. Their mother, Jane, maintained a residence in

Washington, D.C. Georgie moved to Pittsburgh to be close to her sister. Without Roshier's pension and wages to sustain her, Georgie needed a job. In the 1900 U.S. Census, dated June 1, "Georgie A. Creecy" stated that she lived in Pittsburgh, Ward 19, on Hays Street and worked in the house as a servant to James Sloan, a white widower with four children. She was age twenty-four, born in Virginia in May 1876; her race was black, she was a mother of one child, she could read and write, and her marital status was "widowed."[72] She had not heard from Roshier in a long time and didn't know whether he was alive or dead.

In the March 31, 1901 Canadian Census of the Territories, "Roshiar H. Creesy" was enumerated as a resident.[73] With extraordinary impertinence, everything he told the census taker, except for his name, was a lie. He reported that his marital status was single, he had arrived in the Yukon Territory in 1893 and that his nationality was Mexican. Roshier was hitting his stride in spinning tall tales! Another explanation is that he did not wish to be identified as an African American. With his mixed race coloring, he could easily have passed as a descendant of Mediterranean or Spanish blood. Roshier was thriving. He liked his freedom. "A life of freedom and adventure has a fascination which grows rather than diminishes."[56]

Roshier made at least one trip to Seattle during his residency in the Yukon. Rapid progress in transportation had been made between Dawson and the Outside since he arrived in 1898. By August of 1899, a person could take a steamer to Whitehorse, a tram around the rapids, another steamer to Lake Bennett, and the White Pass Railroad to Skagway. The journey from Dawson to Seattle took just thirteen days![64]

Accordingly, more people traveled in and out of Dawson. By the end of 1901, Roshier had returned to Seattle, where he received a letter on November 6, 1901 addressed to "Roshier H. Creecy at 39 Union Block, Seattle, Washington." The letter was from the Department of the Interior, Bureau of Pensions, "Sir, An application for a duplicate certificate No. 808636 has been received and will be considered before the next payment of pension is due."[21]

In an August 8, 1903 census of Dawson, "Roshier Creecy" was listed as a resident, his occupation was gambler and his ethnicity was American.[74, 75] Having not heard from Roshier in a long time, in desperation, Georgie contacted the U. S. consul, who placed the following advertisement in *The Dawson Record* on September 9, 1903. "Missing People Inquired for by Friends. The following is the latest list compiled by the police of missing people inquired for by their friends. Roshier H. Creecy, by the United States consul, Dawson."

Missing People Inquired for by Friends.

The following is the latest list compiled by the police of missing people inquired for by their friends. Roshier H Creecy, by United States consul, Dawson

Advertisement in *The Dawson Record* inquiring after "Roshier H. Creecy," September 9, 1903[71]

While Roshier was exploring the gold fields of the Far North, his son, Nathan, was growing up without him. Years later, Nathan recalled his life in Brookland. In the late 1800s, the area was country. Nathan had a little white bull-dog that herded the cattle on his grandfather's 75-acre ranch in Brookland. "We had a small ranch, my grandfather, Offterdinger, bought cattle and fed them. He was a butcher by trade." Nathan said he was mostly raised by his grandparents. His mother worked all the time at a sales agency, she would "go to stores and take orders." Nathan's job on his grandfather's ranch was to "bring the cattle in, chickens, pigs, feed 'em." Then, his grandfather would sell them. The ranch was 1 mile from the Baltimore and Ohio Railroad that had opened a line in Brookland. Nathan recalled that his grandfather once told him to go to the railroad and "check the box cars and get off the pigs and herd 'em to the ranch, through the fence."[49]

Georgie divorced Roshier. In 1904, she married a Pennsylvania railroad engineer, Lewis George Deskins, in Pittsburgh, Pennsylvania. Their daughter, Jane Elizabeth Deskins, was born in 1906. Although Lewis' job was in Pittsburgh, Georgie spent some time at the Washington, D.C. home as well.

Chapter 6

Eureka Creek Roadhouse

While thousands of prospectors left Dawson for the Nome gold fields, the Klondike gold fields remained a lively place from 1900–1903. There was still gold to be mined, and the increasing number of dredges being brought in bolstered gold production. To keep prospectors in the Yukon, the Canadian government halved the much-hated tax and released its mining claims on creeks, thus opening up more land to prospect.[64] Prospecting reached down to the Indian River and its tributaries, which formed the southern boundary of the roughly 800 square mile Klondike gold fields. Gold had been discovered in the Indian River drainage in 1894, but little effort had been expended in getting it out. As the rich claims on Bonanza and Eldorado Creeks played out, miners roamed south to Indian River. Within the Indian River drainage, 13 miles of claims were staked on Eureka Creek. Ophir, Sulfur, Quartz and Gold Run Creeks were proving rich as well.[56]

In 1904, Roshier Creecy realized his dream and became proprietor of the Eureka Creek Roadhouse. Eureka Creek is located about 70 miles southeast of Dawson, and measures just 10 miles long and 8 feet wide. Eureka Creek enters the Indian River, which flows into the Yukon River. Roshier had much to be hopeful about. In 1902, the commissioner of the North-West Mounted Police reported on the status of gold mining in the Yukon: "The industry of the country is in flourishing condition. Many of the old creeks are being reworked and fresh discoveries are legion. There have been several stampedes during the year . . . This winter there are 1,026 steam plants in operation on the creeks, with 37 of those boilers located on Eureka Creek and its tributaries."[70]

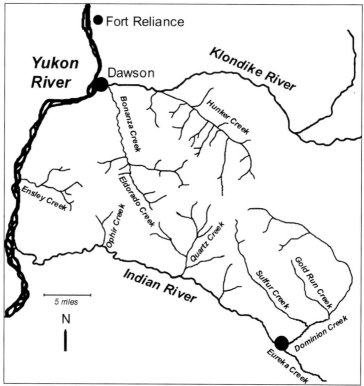

Map of the Klondike and Indian River gold fields showing Eureka Creek, where Roshier Creecy owned a roadhouse, 1904–1906

Roadhouses were often found in the gold fields at the head of rich-producing mines, selling meals at $3.50 each or $12 a day for three hot meals and a bed. While the meals were just staple fare—flapjacks, bacon, beans and tea—they were a welcome respite from hunger acquired through the heavy labor of mining. A roadhouse of that era was a log building containing a long table, benches, and a spruce plank in the corner that served as a bar, behind which sat bottles of liquor on a shelf. A stove in the middle provided heat. A barn housed dog teams and pack horses which often accompanied miners as they traveled throughout the gold fields.

Klondike roadhouse. 1898[53]

In addition to serving miners, roadhouses were convenient quarters from which Mounties carried out their duties while traveling throughout the district. The Mounties inspected roadhouses to make sure that liquor was not being sold without a license. They also collected taxes, conducted fire inspections, acted as postmasters, and served as clerks of the court. As reported by the commissioner of the North-West Mounted Police in 1902, "A good deal of the work on the creeks is serving jury summons, small debt summons, defendant and witness summons, subpoenas and looking for men on warrants."[70] There are several records of the Mounties billeting at Roshier's Eureka Roadhouse. The earliest record dates from a July 9–September 7, 1904 billeting expense report filed by the North-West Mounted Police: "To Creecy, R. H., Eureka, $52."[66]

Roshier's roadhouse business increased with construction of a road from Whitehorse to Dawson. Its route passed right by his doorstep. "At last Dawson is connected to the outside world by a road in winter other than river ice. Its completion, like that of the telegraph line three years ago, is a source of great satisfaction. The road is 323 miles, from Whitehorse across Indian River through the mining centers of Eureka, Bonanza and Eldorado, thence to Dawson."[70]

In August of 1904, another stampede to an Alaskan gold field, the Koyukuk, was broadcast in the *Dawson Daily News*: "Koyukuk a Stayer. This Season Estimated at $300,000 Gross – Two Hundred Men Expected to Spend the Coming Winter There."[76] More Klondikers were going down the Yukon River to mine in Alaska. Roshier kept a watchful eye on the situation, fearing his business would suffer. Another financial blow was the withdrawal of a detachment of Mounties from Eureka Creek

KOYUKUK A STAYER

Most Northerly Camp Will Not Down

REVIEW BY MENZIES

Output This Season Estimated at $300,000 Gross—Two Hundred Men Expected to Spend the Coming Winter There.

Article in the *Dawson Daily News*, August 24, 1904[76]

because a major road was modified: "Detachments permanently withdrawn included Eureka—rendered unnecessary owing to a cut off being made from Lower Dominion to Wounded Moose on the Overland trail."[77]

In May 1905, Roshier made a trip Outside.[5] He closed up his roadhouse and traveled to Dawson, where "R. H. Creary" was reported to stay at the Tanana Hotel, Bar and Pool Hall in the May 23, 1905 issue of the *Dawson Daily News*.[78] When he returned to Eureka Creek in October 1905, it was with shock that he found his roadhouse had been broken into and provisions stolen. There was very little crime in the Klondike. As the commissioner of the North-West Mounted Police noted in his 1903 report, "The most serious crime was supplying liquor to Indians."[77] Roshier wrote a letter of complaint about the break-in and theft to the commissioner, asking the Mounties for help in obtaining restitution, and threatening to take action on his own. A response from the assistant commissioner was dated October 25, 1905 to Mr. R. H. Creecy, Eureka Creek, Y.T.[21]

Dear Sir,

Referring to your complaint that some person or persons unknown have broken into your roadhouse and stolen provisions there from, I beg to inform you I have forwarded your letter to Major Cuthbert for enquiry into the matter. On the arrival of the next patrol from Grand Forks, if you will give them all the information you can we will endeavor to apprehend the guilty parties and put a stop to the thefts. In the meantime, however, I would not advise you to take the law into your own hands, as you suggest, as you would render yourself liable to an action for assault.

Yours truly, Z.J. Worn,

Asst. Commissioner. Comdg. RNWM Police, YT.

On November 21, 1905, Roshier received a second letter from the assistant commissioner.[21]

Dear Sir,

Referring to your complaints regarding thefts of provisions from your cabin, as you are aware, the Police, by my directions, have taken steps to prevent a repetition of the thefts and annoyances you were subjected to and, I would be glad to hear if you have any further cause for complaint.

Yours truly, Z.J. Worn,

Asst. Commissioner. Comdg. RNWM Police, YT.

Perhaps Roshier could see that business at his roadhouse was failing and there was no hope for an improved financial outlook. He knew the Klondike gold fields were playing out for the lone prospector and the only money to be made was by the big corporations operating dredges. It is also possible that Roshier became deeply offended by the break-in and robbery at his roadhouse. For whatever reason, after seven and a half years, he gave up on the Klondike. On January 4, 1906, "R. H. Creecy" gave a forwarding address of Fairbanks, Alaska to Benjamin Craig, a post office worker in Dawson who kept a detailed list of people dying or leaving the Klondike.[79] When he left for Alaska, Roshier was forty years old.

Chapter 7

Bound for Alaska

Klondikers leaving Dawson during winter for gold strikes in Alaska traveled the Yukon River Winter Trail by dog team. At the turn of the twentieth century, the Yukon River Winter Trail was also traversed by mail carriers, freighters, Episcopal priests[80] and a magistrate.[81] The trail followed rivers and creeks as far as the desired direction, then ascended mountains and dropped into valleys, picking up a frozen waterway again as soon as convenient. The trail was dotted with a handful of small communities that had arisen from old trading posts. Interspersed between settlements were roadhouses and shelter cabins, spaced at distances of roughly 10–20 miles apart—the average rate of travel by dog team on wet or dry trail, respectively. If a dog team was run for a long day over a good dry trail, they could cover as much as 40 miles in a day. Judge James Wickersham often traveled the Yukon River Winter Trail to hold court in the Yukon River communities. In a March 4, 1901 entry to his diary, the Judge wrote of meeting miners passing along the trail, "Met many Stampeders from Dawson en route to Nome passing down the river with dog teams."[81] The winter trail held danger from overflow and subsequent freezing. If the unsuspecting traveler fell into a pool of water hidden under a thick layer of snow, his immersed feet could quickly freeze in the sub-zero temperatures. Without a quick fire or change of clothes, he was helpless against a frozen limb, or worse, a frozen death. Despite this danger, travel by dog team was the only option for Stampeders seeking to arrive at fresh gold fields during winter. This 1,000-mile frozen historic route from Dawson to Fairbanks along rivers and across mountain ranges has been commemorated by the annual Yukon Quest International Sled Dog Race since 1984.

In January of 1906, Roshier hitched his dogs to a sled laden with several hundred pounds of dog food (rice and dried bundles of fish), blankets, warm clothes and grub, all wrapped by a tarpaulin, and turned them north on the Yukon River. Just 8 miles downstream from Dawson he slipped by Fort Reliance, an old trading post operated by the Alaska Commercial Company from 1874 to 1886. Trading with the Hän group of native people who lived in the upper Yukon region was abandoned when gold was discovered on the Stewart River, transforming fur trappers into gold miners. The first community Roshier encountered on his journey was Fortymile, so called because it was 40 miles from Fort Reliance. When gold was discovered at Fortymile in 1886, it became a proving ground for gold mining methods in the north.[83] Roshier turned off the Yukon River and onto the Fortymile River, a narrow and winding frozen path in a deep canyon. He followed this for 45 miles, then started climbing to Eagle Summit, an arduous task for both dogs and musher with a heavily loaded sled. The descent into the community of Eagle was gradual. The distance covered from Dawson to Eagle was about 150 miles. Eagle, nestled in a spruce-dominated boreal forest just inside the Alaskan border was established as a trading post in 1874. By 1898, its population was over seventeen hundred and had become a major supply hub to the gold miners of the Klondike. In 1899, the U. S. Government built an army headquarters there, called Fort Egbert, to oversee American interests during the Klondike Gold Rush. Fort Egbert operated as the first station of a telegraph system connecting Alaska with the rest of the nation. Eagle became the first incorporated city in Alaska in 1901, but gold discoveries in Fairbanks and Nome diverted the population, so that only a few hundred people lived there when Roshier passed through.[80, 82, 84]

The next town 160 miles down the trail from Eagle was Circle, located in the Yukon Flats. Roshier followed the Yukon River all the way and likely encountered rough chunks of river ice on this stretch. Circle was established as a trading post by Jack McQuesten with the Alaska Commercial Company in 1893. At Circle, the Yukon River widens into an expanse of twisted channels and islands.[85] Leaving Circle, Roshier picked up Birch Creek, a narrow, winding, cold path subject to overflow. Temperatures could have been at −60°F or colder. He mushed on to Central House, established in 1894 as a roadhouse supplying shelter and food to miners in surrounding creeks. Leaving Birch Creek, he climbed a summit, then down the other side he picked up Eagle Creek, leading to the mouth of Twelve Mile Creek. The trail went steeply up the creek to the summit between the Birch Creek drainage and the Chatanika River drainage. The trail was a "blazed line through the forest of spruce" across Goldstream Valley.[81] Fairbanks arose in view resting on the banks of the Chena River.

Fairbanks began as a trading post established on the banks of the Chena River in the fall of 1901 by E.T. Barnette. Barnette named the trading post Chena City. When gold was discovered by Felix Pedro in the Tanana Hills northeast of Fairbanks in July of 1902, Barnette crafted a plan to drum up business by sending an employee to Dawson to spread the news of the Pedro gold strike. When *The Yukon Sun* published a story of the rich strike in Tanana, *The New York Times* picked up the story and the Tanana gold stampede was on. The town came to be called "Fairbanks" when Judge James Wickersham, appointed to Alaska's Third District by President William McKinley in 1900, ran into Barnette and suggested he name the site in honor of Wickersham's mentor, Senator Charles Fairbanks. During the winter of 1902–1903, about seven to eight hundred people struggled through the bitter cold to reach the Fairbanks Mining District. Barnette over-priced goods at his trading post raising an outcry from the prospectors, who convinced him to sell staples at more reasonable prices. As time went on, prospectors found gold in several creeks around Fairbanks launching a solid economy in the fledgling town. The residents of Fairbanks voted to incorporate in 1903, with E.T. Barnette insisting upon becoming its first mayor. By 1904, Wickersham had moved the seat of the Third Judicial District from Eagle to Fairbanks. By 1905, the town had a church, a hospital and in 1906 a newspaper was launched. When Roshier arrived in Fairbanks in 1906, the town's population was over five thousand people and annual gold production had risen to $6 million dollars.[86]

When Roshier arrived in Fairbanks, mail was delivered by steamers traveling up and down the Yukon River during summer, but in winter, mail arrived by dog team. Mail deliveries were a much-anticipated event and were announced in the newspaper, such as this August 21, 1906 article published in the *Fairbanks Daily Times*: "The next outside mail will be received here upon arrival of the *Lavelle Young*, early next week. The *Lavelle Young* left Dawson this morning, according to today's special from the News' Dawson correspondent."[87] In the October 29, 1906 issue of the *Fairbanks Daily Times*, an announcement from the U.S. postmaster in Fairbanks listed the names of people who had letters waiting for them: "Postmaster Clum has letters for all of these. . . R. H. Creasey."[88]

John Philip Clum (1851–1932) was thought to be just the man to bring order to a fledgling postal system in the Alaska Territory as the Klondike Gold Rush began in 1898. He had previously served as Indian agent for the San Carlos Apache Indian Reservation, then mayor and postal inspector during the silver rush of Tombstone, Arizona in the 1890s. Clum was appointed special commissioner to Alaska and arrived in Skagway on March 26, 1898. He set out on the Chilkoot Pass Trail carrying everything he needed to create a post office: postage stamps, mailbags, postal locks and keys, and postmark tools. Traveling 8,000 miles, he equipped existing post offices and established new ones in the gold fields. From 1906–1909 Clum was postmaster in Fairbanks, Alaska, and his daughter, Caro, served as postal clerk. Residents of the gold rush communities were grateful for his service and showed their gratitude by naming a town on the Chandalar River after his daughter, Caro.[89]

Roshier didn't linger in Fairbanks for long because there were reports of large placer gold discoveries in two mining districts to the north, in the Chandalar and in the Koyukuk. The rush was on, with Roshier joining the throng of hopeful miners who left Fairbanks for creeks to the north.

In the Chandalar, gold was discovered on Big Creek, tributary to the North Fork of the Chandalar River by prospectors exploring east from the Koyukuk. The Chandalar Mining District was created by Judge James Wickersham on August 15, 1906. The district, located 190 miles north of Fairbanks, is the area drained by the Chandalar River and its tributaries. French fur traders with Hudson Bay Company named the Gwich'in native people living along the river "Gens de Large" or "nomadic people," which pronounced in English sounds like Chand-da-large and evolved into the name, Chandalar.[90] When gold was first discovered, there were few routes to the area. Historian William Hunt described the Chandalar as "tough country that needed tough men to exploit it."[91] One route was to travel by steamer up the Yukon River to Fort Yukon, which lies just downriver from the mouth of the Chandalar River. From Fort Yukon, miners used poling boats to carry their supplies up the Chandalar River as far as was navigable, then packed to their claims. Another route was to pack or sled supplies from Coldfoot across the South Fork of the Koyukuk River on the 70-mile Coldfoot-Chandalar Trail.[90, 91] In 1909, four big gold veins were discovered as the source of the placer gold and lode claims were established. Better access to the district was required, so the Alaska Road Commission (established in 1905 to improve roads and trails in Alaska) built a network of trails on which hundreds of miners and freighters tramped.[91, 92] The trails and relief cabins built by the Alaska Road Commission opened up the country to exploration and mining camps, which led to mail service and the establishment of communities.

The Koyukuk Gold Rush of 1906 was to Nolan Creek. Gold was first discovered in the upper Koyukuk area in 1899 by Knute Ellingson. His major gold discovery was on Myrtle Creek, tributary to Slate Creek.[93] Knute and his partners found over $15,000 in gold nuggets and dust in a few weeks, thereby drawing the attention of other prospectors. The Koyukuk Mining District, also known as the Wiseman District, was created and in 1901 its first commissioner, probate judge, and recorder was D. A. McKenzie.

Knute Ellingson and partners at their sluicing operation on Myrtle Creek, 1899. U.S. Geological Survey, F. Schrader[94]

Early prospectors brought supplies by sternwheeler as far as Bettles, 75 miles from the mining camps. From there, people traveling in summer used scows pulled up the shallow

Middle Fork of the Koyukuk River by horses, huskies or poled by hand. The scows needed to carry a year's worth of supplies—1,000 to 1,500 pounds. With no tow trail, horses scrambled along the bank to find footing and progress was slow. Those poling against the current by hand described the work as "torture" as they crossed the river repeatedly to avoid swift water, sand bars or logs.[95] In winter, the round trip from the mining camps to Bettles was made by dog team.

Two horses pull a scow laden with miners and their supplies up the Koyukuk River from Bettles to mining camps near Nolan, 1909. U.S. Geological Survey, A. Maddren[96]

In 1902, in response to growing demand, the Northern Commercial Company built a supply depot upriver from Bettles on Slate Creek. The cluster of cabins came to be called "Coldfoot after prospectors who got that far, then turned back because they got cold feet."[97] After 1902, mining in the area diminished and population sagged, but a surge of new miners flooded the area once again with a discovery of gold on Nolan Creek in 1904. "During the first five years of production, this strike produced more than $800,000 in gold."[97]

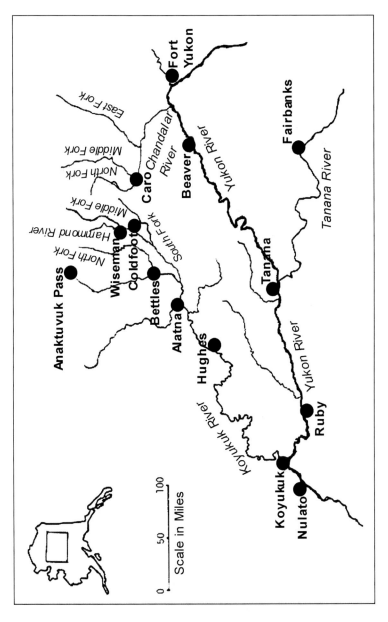

A map of the Chandalar and Koyukuk Rivers, tributaries to the Yukon River, including towns and villages important to the early gold miners

83

Roshier roamed all over the Chandalar and Koyukuk Districts on trails and along creeks. His friend, Tishu Ulen, said of Roshier, "In his early years he traveled all over. He goes over to Chandalar, next year he was in Wild River. He was always on the go, walking, wandering in summer time. In the days he had dogs, he'd take them with him, hiking up one creek, then another."[98]

From December 11–20, 1909, a dedicated census worker with the U.S. Census Bureau made his way on frozen trails throughout the Chandalar District to count people for the 1910 census. The census worker counted a total of 368 persons in the Chandalar District, including a man named "Rabert H. Greasy/Rabert H. Creecy." Throughout his life, Roshier enjoyed playing jokes on census workers by fibbing, for example, changing his birthplace. Roshier told the census worker he was born in Ohio in 1871. The race noted was "black." His home in 1910 was Chandalar, Alaska Territory. He was single, his father's birthplace was Virginia, his mother's birthplace was Ohio, and his occupation was "prospect for gold."

The hardships endured by the Chandalar District **census worker** in December of 1909 are related in the Thirteenth Census of the U.S., Statistics for the Alaska Territory: "The enumerator for the Chandalar District crossed and re-crossed the Arctic Range, traveling above the timberline for 18 hours at each crossing. At no time after he left Fairbanks did the thermometer rise above 30 below zero. Two of his dogs froze to death, and he himself froze portions of his face several times, and at one time dropped into 6 feet of open water, nearly losing his life. He traveled in many places where no white man had ever been before." [90] A total of 103,381 people were counted in the Alaska Territory in 1910, of which 64,356 were white, 36,400 were "Indian," 1,209 were Chinese, 913 were Japanese, 209 were noted as "Negro" and 294 were "Other." Of the 209 Negros counted in the Alaska Territory, 66 were female.[99]

Four thousand miles away, in Washington, D.C., a 1910 U.S. Census worker found Roshier's son, Nathaniel "Crusy," living on Eleventh Street. Nathan was fourteen years old, his race listed as "mulatto." The mother of the household was Georgie Deakins/Deskins, age twenty-nine, race listed as "mulatto." She had been married for six years, and she worked as a cook. Also in the household was Georgie's daughter, Janie Deskins, age three and Georgie's mother, Jane Arnold. Jane was sixty-six, born in 1844 in Virginia, her race listed as "mulatto."

In 1911, Roshier established a base of operations in Wiseman[59] and filed gold mining claims in creeks to the north, including Vermont Creek, tributary to the Hammond River, which flows into the Middle Fork of the Koyukuk River. Gold was discovered on Vermont Creek in 1901. The news of this gold strike made it all the way to Dawson, where on July 1, 1903, the *Dawson Nugget* quoted a miner whom Roshier would soon become partners with, Joe R. Mathews, as saying, "Vermont Creek is the best creek in the country yielding good returns." In 1913, A. G. Maddren, a geologist with the U.S. Geological Survey, described Vermont Creek: "The gravel is about 3 feet thick along Right Fork and the pay streak is narrow due to the constriction of the valley. The shallow placers that continue from Right Fork into Vermont Creek are covered by 6 to 8 feet of muck, and the auriferous gravel is up to 400 feet wide and 4 to 5 feet thick. The gold in Vermont Creek is on and in the top few inches of the bedrock. The gold forms few small nuggets and is mostly fine."[96]

Maddren reported that $172,000 (about 9,050 ounces) was produced from Vermont Creek from 1901 through 1909. "Much if not most of the rich shallow gravel was probably mined out by 1909."[96] Estimated placer gold production of the whole Koyukuk Mining District from 1899 to 1912 was about $2.7 million. "The placer gold is of high grade, $18 to $19 an ounce."[96] Maddren described shallow placer mining in the Koyukuk: "Hand shoveling, sometimes in combination with a little ground sluicing, in the shallow unfrozen stream and bench gravels less than 6 feet deep has been the method by which most of the gold has been mined in this district. . . Deposits of this kind are best suited for immediate development by men whose principal capital is hardihood and willingness to work."[96]

Goods had to be shipped to the Koyukuk region at a cost of 10–20 cents per pound. The annual cost of food and clothing for the average prospector in 1909 was about $1,000. Given the high cost of freight, Maddren surmised: "Under the present commercial conditions, only the richest placers of this district yield returns that are considered an adequate reward. . . A large part of the mining has been done with a relatively low percentage of profit, so low in many instances as to furnish no more than a bare living under the harsh conditions of climate and isolation that characterize this region where only the optimism that is the predominant characteristic of the goldseeker's temperament serves to stimulate many of these men to continued effort year to year."[96]

Having established himself with a gold claim in Alaska, Roshier reached out and contacted his family. His first letter was to his favorite sister, Virginia. In an interview with Virginia's granddaughter, Loma Pointer, Loma reminisced about her family: "Great Uncle Roshier ran away from home when he was young and they [the Creecy family] didn't know where he was for a long time. The next time they heard from him, he was in Alaska." Loma speculated that during Roshier's time, there was "Jim Crow law back in Virginia, but not in Alaska."[2] Roshier also sent a few letters to Georgie, as recalled by Nathan, "My mother corresponded with him." Nathan wrote to his father "once in awhile."[49]

Georgie Deskins and her son, Nathan Creecy, age seventeen, Pittsburgh, Pennsylvania, 1913[21]

Nathan's grandfather, Offterdinger, sold his ranch in Brookland and bought 100 acres near Norfolk, Virginia. "That's when he really brought the cattle in."[49] Offterdinger opened a butcher shop in Alexandria, Virginia. One day, Nathan's grandfather "left for a week, went down to Norfolk, didn't show up, nothing." In May of 1913, they got word that Gustav G. Offterdinger had killed himself.[49] The May 5, 1913 issue of the *Alexandria Gazette* reported: "Offtendinger, the head of a well-known Lynchburg family, committed suicide at his home Saturday night. His family up to that time was under the impression that he went to Washington, D.C. Saturday night for a visit." With the unexpected loss of his grandfather, Nathan and his family left Washington, D.C. for Pittsburgh.

Nathan vividly recalled his "step-father beatin' my behind, try to push me around, and I thought what the hell, and boom, goodbye! Not going to take shit from someone I didn't know, so I left home. Had $25–$30. 'Course I left home when I was a young fella, never contacted nobody, I never wrote to nobody, I didn't want nobody to know where I was at, trying to make my own livin' as best I could. Mother tried to find me."[49] Georgie hired the Pinkerton Detective Agency to look for her son. Nathan never saw his mother again. He traveled by hopping on freight trains and did all kinds of work. "Riding freight trains was against the law, but I did it with old timers. If they caught you, you got 10 days in jail. But I could run! Hitched a freight train to Chicago, worked the stockyards for awhile. Worked the mines in Cripple Creek, Colorado packing water down the tunnels for the miners. I lost my job in Cripple Creek, Colorado, boss come down and tell me, 'Hey you ever got in any trouble back East? Seem to be there's word out to locate you.' I said I don't want nobody to locate me at all. Boss said, 'You better get the hell out of here because cops is comin' here at 10 o'clock this morning'. He got me my money, $9.45, out of Cripple Creek."[49] Nathan had written to his father in Alaska; he was intent on joining Roshier.

Over the next four years, from 1913 to 1916, Nathan worked his way north. "I run into a fella, Charlie, 'Let's go north' he says, 'we'll get better pay.' Then in Butte, Montana I got a job on a ranch as a ranch hand, fed cattle and walked the fence. Then I run into this fella again, Charlie, he says 'Let's go north.' On the rails to Seattle. I didn't have any money, couldn't get a job in Seattle to save my soul." Nathan eventually found work for the Northwestern Steamship Company. He was hired to work on a coal-fired steamship going to Alaska. "First day at sea I got sick."[49] The ship passed through Unimak Pass in the Aleutian Islands, the preferred route between the Pacific Ocean and Bering Sea. Due to the shallow shelf, the ship cast anchor 2 miles offshore of Saint Michael, home to the Yup'ik people. Passengers transferred to smaller steamers to land on the island. Most of the passengers camped out in tents on the island's beach were prospectors, eager to continue their journey into the Alaskan gold fields via the Yukon River, located 80 miles southwest of the island. While they made preparations for the river run, the prospectors traded with the seasoned Yup'ik natives for moccasins, fur mittens and parkas. The Yup'ik had been trading with white men since the first Russians landed on the island in 1833. Naming the island after the archangel, Saint Michael, the Russians established a trading post. In 1897, the U.S. military established a post on the island, which became a major gateway to the gold fields of interior Alaska.

"Got off that ship and I quit. I got $67, this was in 1916. I got a job on a steamer, the *Sarah,* going up the Yukon River, she burned coal or wood."[49] The *Sarah* had been built in 1898 in Unalaska, she was 223 feet in length and weighed 1,130 tons. Nathan fired the boiler and oiled the paddle wheels. "Paddle wheeler, day and night you had to oil the paddle wheels."[49]

The Yukon River steamboat, *Sarah*, 1900–1916, stopped at a wood-yard[47]

Steamboats on the Yukon River heated water in a boiler with wood or coal to create steam, which was piped into the engines under pressure. The engines moved long arms, called pitmans, back and forth. The pitmans connected to each side of a paddlewheel at the stern of the boat and moved the wheel. The slowest wheel revolved twelve to fourteen times a minute. The planks of the wheel dipped into the water and pushed it behind to move the boat forward. While underway, the crew constantly fed wood to the fire. A two-boiler boat used about two cords of wood an hour, around-the-clock. Steamboats had to stop every ten to twelve hours to buy more wood at wood yards operated along the river. The steamboats also had to stop often to clean their boilers because scum from the muddy river built up quickly and the boilers had to be washed down. On the lower Yukon River steamboats could travel as fast as 7 miles per hour upriver, but above the confluence with the Tanana River, the Yukon became more treacherous with shifting and shallow sandbars and progress upriver was slower. Steamers had two or three decks. The lowest deck housed fuel, boilers, the engine and freight. The next deck housed a dining area ringed by small cabins. The highest deck had crew cabins and the pilothouse, in which a huge pilot wheel controlled giant rudders at the stern of the boat.[100]

Nathan got off the *Sarah* in Nulato, a village located on the Yukon River just below the mouth of the Koyukuk River. He took a scow up the Koyukuk River to Wiseman. Nathan had sent a letter to his father from Pittsburg, and addressed the letter to Roshier in Wiseman, saying that he was coming to Alaska to meet him. But, Nathan had taken several years to reach Wiseman. In the meantime, Roshier had heard of a gold strike and stampede at Wild Lake, located about 60 miles north of Bettles (later renamed Old Bettles), and wanted to try his luck there. Roshier left Wiseman and set up a second base of operations in Bettles. What a disappointment to Nathan, to travel thousands of miles, over several years, expecting to find his father in Wiseman, only to discover that Roshier was in Bettles! There was nothing else for him to do but to turn around and go back down the Koyukuk River.

"From there [Wiseman] I couldn't get nothin'. I had a couple hundred dollars. I buy myself a small boat with a

Evinrude motor, got to Ruby. I stayed there, they had a stampede out there 20 miles, some guy hit some money out there. So, I stayed in Ruby for the winter."[49] Ruby was a gold rush town, established in 1911, and hit its peak population of close to three thousand people before 1918.

Nathan got word to Roshier in Bettles that he was overwintering in Ruby, and they agreed to meet in what was then called Alatna, located on the south bank of the Koyukuk River. (In 1938, the town's name was changed to Allakaket, the old Athabascan name for the Saint John's-in-the-Wilderness Episcopal Mission, established there in 1906. Inupiaq people moved across the Koyukuk River to the north bank, and assumed the name of Alatna for their community).

During a really cold spell in December of 1916, Nathan made his way from Ruby upriver to Tanana. He left Tanana for Alatna in the company of two men, J. Corbett and C. Goodwin. Along the trail there was a report of −68°F. Nathan suffered from frostbite on his journey. As Nathan later recalled, "I come across [from Tanana] with a couple of fellas, we only had five dogs. I was snowshoeing. The mail company had already come through; we were trying to follow the dog team trail left by the mail company. . . They left me at camp [with the gear and dogs] and went on into town. Poor old me, I didn't know anything, finally got tired of waiting, turned the dogs loose and followed them on snowshoes into town. Went to the roadhouse, that's where the fellas were. In Alaska, you wait for somebody for so long and nobody shows up, you say the hell with it. I'm going to get out of here! That's all there is to it."[49]

The January 30, 1917 *Fairbanks Daily News-Miner* mentioned their journey in a report by Deputy Marshal E. D.

Heppenstall, who had traveled to Allakaket to investigate a recent suicide. "On arriving here we found Jas. Corbett, Chas. Goodwin and N. H. Creecy, who had left Tanana December 30, 1916. Caught during the cold spell between the 1st and the 7th [of January]. Had a very difficult trip. Creecy froze three fingers on right hand. Miss Pumphrey [missionary nurse] is caring for him. Two middle fingers may have to be amputated at the middle joint. Also one heel slightly frozen. Goodwin has one heel slightly frozen. Mr. Corbett got through with only a blistered face."[101]

Nathan described meeting his father, who had come down from Bettles as a passenger in the sled of the mail carrier and his big dog team. "That's the first time I met him. There was no affection when we met. So, he came and picked me up. The [mail carrier and his] dog team turned around and headed back to Bettles, they'd gone. But we had the trail to follow. We left early that morning on snowshoes. It took us all that day and half into the night to get to Bettles. I was so tired, when we got into Bettles, I was so tired. And he'd snowshoe way ahead of me, then turn around and come meet me to see if I was still comin', he kept that close enough to me, then I'd be right behind him for awhile, then I guess he'd look and see me and then he'd turn around and come back and meet me. 'What the hell's the matter, can't you keep up?' That's all he said." Roshier had a cabin in Bettles, and "we stayed in that cabin the rest of the winter."[49] Roshier asked Nathan how Georgie was, what she was doing. But he never explained to his son why he took off. That unanswered and lingering question had been a burden to Nathan as a child, and he confided later in life, that it bothered him as an adult for some time.[49]

In 1917, the town of Bettles had diminished in size since it was first established around 1898 by fur trader and store owner, Gordon Bettles. His store supplied prospectors during the 1898 Koyukuk Gold Rush. Bettles was the northern terminus of a steamboat line and a little town grew around the store, including a post office and roadhouse.[102] Nathan recalled that when he ". . . arrived in Bettles, there were 40–50 people, natives, 8–10 white people. Natives were educated at the mission [Saint John's-in-the-Wilderness Episcopal Mission] and good gamblers too, stud and draw poker. All night long, natives would gamble off boots, traps, dogs, furs, anything. Father came home one night with five dogs he won in a poker game. Natives drank. They had this hops, made beer."[49] Natives that inhabited the area around Bettles, or came to trade there, included Koyukon Athabascan native people and Inupiaq native people from the Arctic villages of Kobuk, Selawik and Anaktuvuk Pass.[102]

Chapter 8

Wild Lake

In the spring of 1917, a prospector named Joseph "Joe" R. Mathews asked Roshier to work his claims for him on Jay and Rye Creeks, near Wild Lake. Joe Mathews was born in Ontario, Canada in 1864 to immigrant German parents. In 1897, he arrived in Skagway and by 1902 had traveled to Coldfoot to look for gold. Joe had pretty good luck at finding gold in the Koyukuk region. In 1903, he discovered gold on Spring Creek. "In the years 1904 to 1912, Joe Mathews mined out about $22,500."[103] Joe also owned a Discovery Claim on Emma Creek, mined on Summit Creek and in 1912, he had staked Discovery Claim on Jay Creek and claim no. 1 below Discovery, which projected 500 feet into the valley of Rye Creek.[103, 104] Prospectors flocked to the Wild River area and quite a community formed there, named "Mathews." The May 19, 1915 issue of the *Fairbanks Daily Times* reported, "Democrat Club, 96 strong, formed on Wild River at Mathews on April 20. . . Request post office at Mathews."[101]

When he was not out prospecting, Joe lived in his cabin in Bettles and worked as crew on a steamer. According to the July 1, 1903 issue of the *Dawson Nugget*, "J. R. Mathews left Bettles as Chief Engineer on the *Rock Island*." The steamer, *Rock Island*, plied the Yukon and Koyukuk Rivers for the Northern Navigation Company. Nathan Creecy described Joe, "Joe was a nice guy, a big husky guy, German descent. He was mostly around Bettles, go to the commercial store, go back to his mining camp and stay up there the whole winter. Joe used to go prospect, would be gone a week to 10 days from his cabin. You couldn't find him, just knew Joe had gone. You could see he took his pack. Joe didn't care too much for dogs, more on foot, snow shoes. He'd pack 40–50 pounds. He didn't have much to say. The only time he'd do any talking was when he was half drunk."[49]

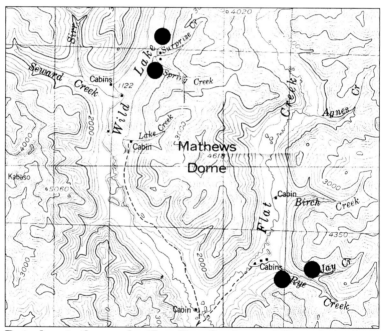

Dots denote the creeks (Jay, Rye, Spring and Surprise) where Roshier Creecy was known to have mined for gold in the Wild Lake area, 1917–1933[105]

Jay and Rye creeks are located in the Wild Lake area (also called Clear Lake), about 60 miles above the Arctic Circle in the southern foothills of the Brooks Range. Jay and

96

Rye Creeks flow into Flat Creek, a tributary to Wild River, a tributary to the Koyukuk River, which flows past Bettles. Miners traveled up and down Wild River in spring and fall to access supplies in Bettles or their properties in the Wild Lake area, although Reed described the navigation of Wild River as "arduous."[103]

Nathan explained: "Father didn't go to Wiseman no more, we went to Jay Creek, Rye Creek, out of Bettles. Oh hell, that was a real stampede! You talk about guys in there! Wild Lake was up from Rye Creek and they had a stampede over there, some guy hit some gold."[49]

In 1937, Irving Reed photographed the Wild Lake area where Roshier prospected, "Looking down Flat Creek from right limit of Rye Creek to Hardnut Mountain."[103]

Initially, Roshier and Nathan worked for wages, but as they became friends, Joe gave them one of his claims so that he would have company. Eventually, Roshier and Nathan staked their own claims. Nathan detailed their time mining.

My father and I worked the claim that Mathews had, to give us a chance. Dynamite, shovel dirt in a sluice box. We worked for Joe, he paid us. I didn't see much gold, every once in awhile a small nugget worth about $8 to $14 or so. Then, Mathews give my old man and me a half a claim up Rye Creek and Jay Creek half way. Where Jay Creek run into Rye Creek, that's where my father and I, we hit some good color. That's where we cleaned up $1,600, but we used $40 to $50 worth of dynamite. We'd drill by hand. Push the stick in, put your cap, light the fuse, you got to get the hell out of there. A lot of big boulders, underneath we got a little bit of gold, drifted downstream underneath the rock. After we blew it out, we could take shovel and sluice box it. Sluice box made of whip saw lumber. Riffles made out of cottonwood limbs four to six in the middle. You shovel the mud in there and as the water comes down it gradually washes the mud away. You take the riffle thing out of there, and then shut the water off and find your gold on the bottom. We went after quartz gold, didn't give a damn about the fine stuff, so didn't have a burlap bag to hold that fine stuff. My father and I, we staked one claim below Mathews and then we staked one claim below the canyon. They found gold down there, but at that time, it didn't seem to pay, by the time you packed your wood in, your grub and gear, a lot of labor. You couldn't get no strata to follow, just gold quartz sprinkled in spots.

Our log cabin was down at the mouth of Rye Creek. Mathews' cabin was a little ways up. [To build a log cabin] cut out a notch in the logs, chink in the cracks with mud and moss. Dirt floor, no windows, no doors. Door will be skin, blanket, old piece of canvas. Father was pretty tight [thrifty]. Bunks were made out of small logs. Tie it up with string or hide, we didn't have nails or wires.[49]

The men laid moss over the log bunk as a makeshift mattress, then sleeping bags were laid on top. The stove was a 20 gallon barrel with 3 pound coffee cans cut to fit together as a stove pipe. The cabin was smoky, because the connections between cans were not tight. When it got too smoky, they were forced to lie on the floor to breathe the fresher air near the ground. The stove was used for cooking and heating. Steaks were cooked on top of the stove but roasts were placed directly in the fire. The outside of the meat burned, but the inside was medium rare. Nathan said that over time, Roshier built two cabins on Rye Creek and one in Bettles.

"In summer, worked all day and night, pick and shovel work, shoveling about 10 feet each side of the box, up the stream. Got nuggets in the gravel. Found some quartz, gold in the rock. Small pieces. Back then, gold was $19 to $20 an ounce. We had a scale, split the gold, 50:50."[49]

Nathan said that he and his father had pretty good luck on Jay Creek: "We cleaned up that fall just before it started freezin', I think we cleaned up about $3,000 to $4,000."[49] Wanting to focus his gold-seeking efforts in the Wild Lake area, Roshier left for Wiseman to sell his claim on Vermont Creek. Nathan described the journey: "From Jay Creek, cross by foot to Wiseman. Make it in one day in summer, leave early in the morning. Get across North Fork [Koyukuk River] with a raft, get across there, you go down the hill."[49]

On October 11, 1917, Roshier sold his claim, "One above Discovery on Vermont Creek, a tributary of Hammond River, also cabin contents, sluice boxes, etc." to James Traill for $250. The sale was officiated by T. B. Wright, commissioner, and witnessed by H. S. Wanamaker and G. W. Huey.

Portions of the bill of sale for Roshier's gold mining claim on Vermont Creek to James Traill, October 11, 1917[21]

Back in Bettles, Roshier went into the Northern Commercial store and expressed his opinion about America's entry into World War I, which had occurred several months earlier, on April 6, 1917. He was critical of President Woodrow Wilson leading the United States into war after he had promised to keep the country out of it. Roshier cared deeply about conflict, evidenced by the magazine and news clippings found among his effects after his death.

> They are real people. They love—they laugh. They have codes of honor. They enjoy life just as do we. They have babies. They have their worries and their joys. . . . *TOMORROW—Let's go to church and pray for them. Let's pray God to stop the march of that dread monster WAR.*

"It is a crime that men such as the great artists of France are in the field being shot at—and shot—when they could and should be at home advancing the world's civilization instead of tearing it down and being cut down themselves with bullets.

"Modern warfare is merely a question of the best guns, the most modern war-machinery and -implements, and the longest purse.

Magazine clippings relating to World War I found among Roshier's effects after his death[21]

Roshier's opinions got him into trouble with the law, as recounted years later by Harry Leonard, Koyukuk gold miner, who was a friend of Roshier's. "Creecy, during the First World War, Creecy was down at the N. C. store, there was a bunch of them in there, and Wilson was the president then, you know, and they was talkin' around there about the war, you know, and Creecy gave them his opinion. Told them that President Wilson ought to have his ass rubbed with a corn cob! They had a U.S. Marshal there, you know, a marshal was the law and he arrested Creecy for saying such a thing! During those days, the marshal was paid for each person he arrested and brought to jail in Tanana. They took Creecy to Tanana. He spent some time that winter in jail in Tanana, which he reckoned was cheaper than putting up his own operation."[5]

When Roshier was called pro-German for his criticism of the president's war policy, Roshier replied, "When my country does wrong I'm going to criticize. That's what the real hundred percent American will do."[106]

Nathan was also arrested. In the November 14, 1917 issue of the *Fairbanks News-Miner*, a short article stated, "R. H. Creecy, a black at Bettles, arrested for seditious utterances. The accused made statements against President Wilson and severely criticized government actions in carrying on the war. Nathaniel Creecy, his son at Bettles, arrested for failing to register for military service; he is reported to be 24 years old and to have refused to register."[101]

From the very outbreak of **World War I**, President Wilson pursued non-intervention. The president was re-elected in 1916 largely on a platform of peace. However, it became apparent that the German Empire was committed to unrestricted submarine warfare and several American ships were sunk by the Germans in February and March 1917. Then, the British Secret Service revealed the German Empire's conspiracy with Mexico to invade the U.S. Wilson called for a war to end all wars and Congress declared war on April 6, 1917. WWI was unprecedented in levels of destruction because of new technologies, chemical warfare, and the tactical blunder of trench warfare. When the Allied Powers claimed victory in November 1918, more than 16 million people, soldiers and civilians had died.

The population in the Alaska Territory declined due to the withdrawal of young men into WWI. In 1900, the population was 63,592, but by 1920 had declined to 55,036. Gold miners threw down their picks and shovels to sign up for

---

the military, leaving small mining towns nearly deserted. The war's increased demand for copper created a boom in the copper industry. Alaska's salmon industry also benefited when the military purchased canned salmon to feed the troops. The Territorial Legislature passed laws to punish seditious acts and draft avoidance. After the war ended, copper and salmon export prices fell, creating an economic downturn.[107, 108, 109]

Having reunited later at their cabin on Rye Creek, Roshier and Nathan set about surviving the rest of the winter. The Koyukuk average low temperature is 11°F, and gets down to –60°F or colder in January.[49] Average snow fall is 85 inches. Roshier and Nathan lived primitively, but had food and shelter. Nathan described what their life was like. "In winter, dressed in a [hoary marmot] parky with wolverine fur around the hood, frost and ice never stay, never stick to it. Wolverine got a good price, $125, even $200. Cure it with brown soap and willow leaves." When it got really cold, dogs were brought in to help keep them warm while they slept.[49]

For food, they hunted wild game. Nathan said they didn't have a .22 rifle. All they had was a Winchester .30-.30 carbine rifle and a 12 gauge shotgun. "Didn't get ducks or geese, very few fish. We got a caribou every other month, one moose, 14 to 15 Dall sheep. A male wild sheep was tough, but the female or young sheep were good eating. The mountain sheep were shrewd, could smell you a mile away, but they'd be in bunches. If you get into the mountains, crawl up where they can't smell you, see you, you could get four or five at a time if you got close enough. Sheepskin worth $25. Sell at trading posts. We got two black bear, weighed 150 to 200 pounds. Boil, roast, fried. Meat is sweet, bear eating these blueberries. We got one grizzly bear, 400–500 pounds. Snared rabbit around the mouth of Rye Creek. Dig a hole 2 feet, put a log across the hole and hang the meat. When meat freezes, –20°F, nothing can eat it." Nathan said they made hardtack. "Mixed flour, water, baking powder and fried it in a pan—that was our bread." On occasion, they'd go into Bettles to get grub at the N. C. store. The road commission had put up relief cabins, every 10 or 12 miles on the Wild River Trail.[5] "One and a half days to get to Bettles. Got five to seven dogs, got to help the dogs, they can't pull a loaded sled." Sometimes they would buy whitefish from Athabascans: ". . . the meat is white, but bones! Ate lots of it baked or boiled."[49]

On October 9, 1978, Nathan Cristini modeled mukluks and a wolverine-ruffed parka he brought Outside when he left Alaska, and stored in a trunk for fifty-four years.[21]

There were few leisure activities during winter. Nathan said he played a harmonica. His father smoked a pipe, drank, played cards and read. Nathan reminisced about Roshier.

He drank, everyone did, but he didn't get drunk often. Old man bought some apricots one year. Boy, he must have bought $40–$50 worth of apricots, made this

104

brandy out of it. Boil the damn stuff on a wood stove outside, put it through copper pipes, run it down through the snow, hell you'd be surprised. He traded it for fish, dogs. He gambled, but that's about all. Joe Mathews and my dad would play poker, cards are dirty and worn out, but they'd still play poker. They'd make some apricot brandy and get drunk and play cards with small nuggets, two or three. The colors on the cards were faded, but 15 miles from a trading post, where you goin' to get anything else? Nothing's cheap in Alaska. My dad and Mathews talked a little about politics and stuff, they'd get a paper, it would be a month behind, you only get mail once a month into Bettles. Then whoever went into Bettles, take it round Rye or Jay Creek. Give an educated Indian so much to take your mail to you, otherwise it laid around in the store until you came to pick it up. N. C. [store] controlled everything. Dad was liberal in his thinking. He was a hard worker, he had brains. Nobody talked about how old a person was, or where they came from or what they thought, all that mattered was the gold scale.[49]

In his interview, Nathan was asked if Roshier liked to read? "Hell, that's all he did! I had to go out and cut the wood, pack it in. Read, read, read books, magazines. The old man never talked, never told me nothin' about his time in Dawson, all the time read, read, read. Damned old books, 1898, 1901, 1902, Wild West stories. Always readin'! He'd cut wood a little bit, then he'd read. Then he'd go out and hunt a little bit, come back with one or two rabbits, or a porcupine, something like that. Skin it, then have something to eat. My dad would read by two candles at night stuck on the bunk post. No table. Cooked the stuff and ate it sittin' on his bunk."[49] Nathan said that the one thing his father talked to him about was mining, but otherwise, Roshier didn't tell him anything about his past. Later in life, Nathan remarked that he didn't know anything about Roshier's family in Virginia.[49]

Father and son did winter drift mining on creeks near the cabin as well as prospecting in drainages several miles away. They built fires to thaw the frozen ground. "Put pieces of logs, build a fire, 3 by 4 feet. Shove a roast into the ashes under the logs. Get down a foot, prospect holes, burn all day long, go down 8 inches or a foot. Take you 10 days to get 5 feet. We prospected over towards Porcupine River but we never found anything. Drifting with wood fires, sink a hole 75 feet along a creek, it was -5° or -10° F." The thawed earth was brought to the surface and would be sluiced in spring. "My father went by himself prospecting by Clear Lake [Wild Lake], but I didn't go with him, stayed at the cabin. We had a lot of meat, flour, sugar." When Roshier would take off prospecting in winter, he'd take "a parka, bacon, beans, shovel, .30-.30 carbine, you get a rabbit to eat."[49]

Nathan speculated, "If I'd had heavy equipment in 1918, I'd have made some money! All I had was a pick and shovel, wear the shovel out!" Tools were sharpened by using the fire as a forge and then tempering them in the snow. "Take a pick, put it in the fire, heat it, take a sledge hammer and keep pounding it on a rock, that's how we made it sharp. Take the wooden handle off, use mittens. After that, stick the pick in the snow."[49] They always had snow around them, even in summer. "Snow don't melt in the mountains, around Jay Creek, Rye Creek. Patches along the creek beds."[49]

In his interview, Nathan was asked if there were many native people in the area? "No natives 'round Jay or Rye Creek. They didn't go around mining. If you had freight to bring up the river, they'd haul it for pay. They went hunting and you could buy meat from them. But around mines, no, very few Indians. They were more hunting and trapping."[49]

Nathan described a custom of the Far North when a person died in winter. "When white people died, wrap them in caribou skin, dig down 2–`3 feet, pile rocks on top. Indians, wrap them up in fur and put them in a tree. Next spring, you could smell; by next fall, couldn't smell nothing."[49]

Nathan was asked in his interview if he experienced racial discrimination during his time gold mining at Wild Lake? He replied that no, color didn't matter out there. "Food firewood and gold, that's what the miners cared about."[49]

In the spring of 1918, Roshier and Nathan sluiced earth that had been brought up to the surface from their winter mining efforts. The men were only after gold nuggets and quartz gold, no flakes. They used oil of citronella to keep mosquitoes at bay. "Wear those nets over your hat, get hot." Their provisions were supplemented with a few wild fish, "You had only 6–7 weeks, then everything froze up." Nathan explained that natives would catch salmon, split them in half, dry them in the sun, and sell bales of it, twelve to fourteen fish in a bale. "Sell it to the trading post. Run around $8–10 a bale. You could feed the fish bales to the dogs. If you run out of fish, buy tallow in a can, feed that to the dogs." They foraged for food, "picked blue berries, cranberries, cook 'em a little bit." In the afternoons, storms would occur and fresh snow could fall on the mountains. "August sees the most rainfall."[49]

In the fall of 1918, Nathan found a new best friend in Sammy Hope. "He was like a brother." Sammy was an Inupiaq native born about 1881 near Point Barrow.[110] "We got a grub stake, $100 each, and went hunting. We had a nine-dog team, went hunting for a month. Got sheep, one moose, two caribou, fox, got $300–$400 dollars for the meat. Split the money. Ate beans, flour, sugar, put a rabbit in, dried fruit, powdered eggs. Had a canvas tent and stove, coffee can for a stove pipe. Sammy drank tea, not coffee."

Nathan and Sammy also made some extra money trapping. "My father didn't trap, but I did. Very few wolves around Jay or Rye creeks." To find fur animals they went north toward Point Barrow. "Trapped three wolves in the mountains. Got some wolverines in steel traps, snow shoeing all the time. Get the skins to make a few dollars."[49] Nathan commented that bullets at that time cost 15 cents apiece. "In the fall, walk into the mountains 10 to 12 miles, look for game. If you run out of bullets, or miss, you got nothing to eat." Nathan froze his hand, an ever present and common danger of wintering in the Arctic. The nearest help was in Wiseman, so he went there and stayed ten days. "My hand swelled up, they cut off the dead flesh, put in a few stitches. Bunked at Martin Slisco's rooming house."[49]

When the year 1919 arrived, Nathan decided he had had enough of mining in the wilderness. Although he and his father had "cleaned up" a few times, "the gold cleanup had to be used for the winter and spring grubstake. By the time you bought a grubstake [from the N. C. store] for the next winter, what the hell did you have left?" Nathan left his father that winter. They never saw each other again. "When I left my father in Bettles, I had five dogs, went to Tanana. I had to follow the mail team. Mail man was ahead of me. He was a white man, had a contract to haul mail up once a month. There were cabins along the trail."[49]

In spring when the river ice broke up, Nathan took a steamer down the Yukon River and got a job working at Carlisle Fish Packing Company of Seattle and Cordova, canning and salting barrels of salmon. "The boss there said, 'Creecy, that name sounds like Greasy, you don't want that! I'm goin' to change your name to Creastino!'" [49] After that, Nathan went by Creastino, Creastini, or Cristini. From June 15–September 12, he made $440, but he spent $90 at the company store, so he walked away with $350.

In the fall, Nathan worked his way back up the Yukon River on a steamer and landed in Fairbanks where he stayed until 1924. In Fairbanks, he got a job working for Thomas H. Gibson at Gibson Auto Stage Line. He drove a Ford truck ferrying freight and people between neighboring areas, as well as Valdez, Seward and Dawson. He had to carry his own gasoline with him. He stayed in roadhouses, where a room cost $1.50, and breakfast eggs and meat cost $1.00.The truck he drove had hidden panels, behind which he would stash whiskey bought in Dawson to bring in illegally to Fairbanks. So, Nathan became a bootlegger.[49]

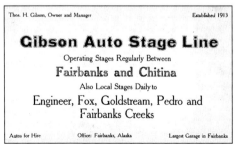

Place of employment for Nathan Creastino, 1920–1924 [21]

Alcohol sales to Alaskan natives by Russians in the 1700 and 1800s was a routine trading tool the Russians used to obtain furs. Following purchase of the Alaska Territory by the United States, from 1867–1877 the War Department prohibited the shipment of beer and wine into Alaska, however the army stationed in Sitka largely ignored the law. Control of alcohol in Alaska fell to the Treasury Department from 1877 to1884. The Treasury Department legalized the importation and sale of beer and wine but prohibited distilled spirits. During these decades of "control," natives and prospectors manufactured homebrew, sometimes called "hootchenoo." In 1884, Alaska's civil government was formed and prohibited all alcohol, but by 1887 a law justifying the sale of alcohol for "sacramental purposes" was passed. The civil government made little effort to enforce the prohibition of alcohol. Saloons operated and druggists sold liquor for "medicinal purposes." In 1892, oversight of alcohol became confused between the territorial governor, who issued permits for its sale, and the Internal Revenue Service, which issued tax stamps to liquor dealers. By 1899, the confusion was sorted out and licensed liquor sales were legal in Alaska. License fees provided funds to build and operate town infrastructures. In 1918, fervor for abstinence ran high and Alaskans voted to enact the "Bone Dry" law, two years before passage of the Eighteenth Amendment. Nonetheless, the importation, manufacture, sale and use of alcohol was widespread, with bootleggers operating brisk businesses until passage of the Twenty-First Amendment in 1933, repealing prohibition.[111]

Nathan made friends and enjoyed his time in Fairbanks. By 1924, Nathan was twenty-eight years old and ready to leave Alaska. Before he left, his employer, Thomas Gibson, wrote him a recommendation letter, dated September 29, 1924:

> Nathan Creastino has been in our employ the past four years as repair man and we have found him to be a very ambitious worker. As to habits, we would not find anything that would not satisfy any person as he certainly is a good, upright and steady man being right on the job at anything you put him at, he has not missed any time since he has been in our employ.[21]

Nathan Creastino at Gibson's Garage, Fairbanks, Alaska, circa 1924[21]

On October 12, 1924, "Nathan Creastino" sailed on the *SS Alaska* from Seward to Seattle, Washington.[21] Nathan went to San Francisco and sold some of his gold nuggets there. He eventually married and settled down in Reno, Nevada where he assumed the name of "Nathan Cristini" and passed as a man of Italian ancestry.[49]

For the next ten years after Nathan left, from 1920–1930, Roshier primarily mined in the Wild Lake area, however he was known to travel extensively throughout the upper Koyukuk River drainage. In the 1920 U.S. Census, "R. H. Creecy" lived in the Koyukuk, he was age fifty, said he was born in Georgia. His race was black, marital status was widower, he owned his own house, and was able to read and write. His occupation was mining placer gold. Years later, Roshier told his friend Harry Leonard stories about his time at Wild Lake. Harry relayed, "Joe Mathews, he had money to buy food that most miners considered a luxury. Creecy was over at ol' Mathew's cabin one time and Joe says, 'Well, I think I'll give the dogs a bunch of eggs tonight' and Creecy says 'Jeez, I haven't seen an egg in a year or so!'"[112] Roshier and Harry would gossip about the people at Wild Lake. Harry remembered, "At that Flat Creek they had quite a stampede in there and started a sort of town there. Some of them "sports" [prostitutes] moved in there and put in houses, one of the sports put up the money for that drill for Fred Swift, sunk like 300 feet they went down. The hooker that gave Fred Swift the money for that drill was named 'Nosy' because part of her nose was gone, she was a colored girl. The drill was on the Wild River and they took it to the South Fork and stayed there."[112] Harry remembered the people he met at Wild Lake on his cross-country tramping. "Must have been seven or eight there anyway . . . Jim Murphy was there, and Frank Smith and his wife, his nephew, Joe Smith and his wife, then there was Sammy Hope and Ludie Hope and [their adopted son] Henry, Creecy and Dunphy and Joe Mathews was over there at the lake."[5]

In the winter of 1924, on one of Roshier's forays, he met Margaret (Mardy) and Olaus Murie, renowned naturalists.

Olaus and Mardy Murie, newlyweds, 1924[113]

Mardy and Olaus had just married in the village of Anvik and were traveling in the Koyukuk region, as part of Olaus' work with the U.S. Biological Survey. They had stopped at Roy King's Fox Farm and Roadhouse. Mardy wrote in her memoir: "We leave Bettles and hope to get to King's, 19 miles, the only roadhouse between here and Wiseman." They had just come over a difficult trail and had explained to their host, Roy, that they were a little tired. Mardy's memoir continues:

Roy exclaimed, "Why that's the worst trail in Alaska right now. My goodness, you must be about dead, both of you. You lie down in your same old bunk, missus, I'll hurry with dinner. This is Bill [Roshier] Creecy."

In the doorway a giant figure was pulling off a red cap. We had heard about Bill Creecy up above. A mulatto, he was a veteran of many campaigns with Uncle Sam's troops, and now was a miner. He came in slowly, gazing bashfully at me, and regarding me timidly as I slipped on dry moccasins and began to brush my hair.

"You a cheechako, ma'am?"

"Oh heavens no, I was raised in the country!"

"Oh dats all right den. You unnerstan' us ole sourdoughs den. I'se afraid you was some city lady."

He heaved a sigh of relief and began eagerly taking part in the rapid conversation going on, Marcel [Sheehy/Sheely] continuing his monologue of "By gar, dat's a tough trail for a lady to come over, my dat's terreeble!" . . . Dinner was a gala affair, such a happy reunion, so much news to relate, so many questions to ask and answer. Here were a French Canadian [Marcel], a mulatto old-time Alaskan [Roshier], an American Hoosier Alaskan [Roy] with a good meal, a bright room, and an admiring audience of two newcomers [Mardy and Olaus] who had never heard any of the stories before. Such an entertainment comes few times in a lifetime, and cannot be retold properly.[114]

According to Harry Leonard, "Creecy had a humorous and witty side to him but didn't show these traits to many people."[5] Roshier also liked to play practical jokes and took special delight in irritating U.S. District Commissioner Charles Irish. One such joke was retold by Harry Leonard. "In 1928, Creecy mined way up Flat Creek, up toward the head of it, in the Wild River area. There was quite a few at the lake at that time, oh, half a dozen or more, Sammy Hope, Frank Smith (he came over to Wiseman). Guys from the lake, they had a trail that they went down to Old Bettles to get grub. Anyway, Creecy had left Flat Creek with his dogs for Bettles. Along the trail he decided to play a practical joke, so he left a note on the trail saying he was out of grub and about to give up. One of them comin' down picked up the note and took it on down to Bettles. They sent the note to Wiseman and ol' Irish, the U.S. Commissioner in Wiseman, hitched up his dogs and went to Bettles hoping to find Creecy along the trail. Long ways they had to go to Bettles, you know. Irish didn't find him in Bettles, so he went on to Flat Creek. There he found Creecy in his tent, who said it was a little joke. [Laughter] Mad!!? Oh!! It was just one of Creecy's jokes."[5] The incident was reported in the *Fairbanks Daily News-Miner*, in an article dated January 19, 1928. "In order to play a 'joke' R. H. Creecy, Koyukuk prospector, left a note on the Wild River trail saying, 'My days are short and they are passing. I am looking for a place to die.' He was given full opportunity to explain his joke when a search party found him alive and well after making a 100-mile trip, much of it over unbroken trail and at a cost of several hundred dollars. Creecy's brand of humor was strongly condemned by the government officials and while there is probably no way in which Creecy can be punished by law, public opinion in the Koyukuk will undoubtedly be even more effective."[101]

According to Harry Leonard[5], Roshier prospected all over the Koyukuk area, "Creecy had been on every creek but never found a lot of gold." He went to areas that had been previously mined and used the sluice boxes left by the previous miners. "All he had to do was to shovel some dirt into the boxes and catch what others had missed." In summer of 1927, Roshier decided to explore Surprise Creek, also known as Summit Creek, a small stream located about 3.5 miles north of the south end of Wild Lake. He had heard that in 1904 a man named Jack Lamont had found gold there. In fact, Jack was reported to have made $6 a day.[103] After Jack, Joe Mathews mined Summit Creek. U.S. Geologist, Irving M. Reed, documented in his report, "Reconnaissance of Upper Koyukuk Region", that "The booming method of mining was used often on Surprise Creek." Miners would build a small dam across the creek using rocks and let water back up behind it. When the rocks were removed, the rush of water would,

". . . wash off the fine material in the creek bed, leaving behind any large rocks. These would then be stacked on the creek bank. The washes would be repeated until the lower 3 feet of pay gravel, lying on bedrock, was exposed. This material was then washed through a sluice box and any gold recovered. A dam could produce about three splashes per hour when sufficient water was available. As a boomed cut progressed upstream, pay gravel was protected by a carefully laid pavement of schist slabs. After sufficient gravel was

116

uncovered for a season's work, the slabs were pulled up and the gravel washed."[103]

Roshier likely built a few rock dams, created some splashes, and shoveled dirt into the old sluice boxes left there by Jack Lamont and Joe Mathews. In Reed's notes he stated, "In 1927, R. H. Creecy re-staked the whole creek. Creecy mined in his upper cut about 350 feet of streambed. His workings were not over 6 feet wide. The lower end of these workings is about 2,400 feet from the lake. Also, Creecy and others before him mined out a lower cut about 500 feet long and not over 15 feet wide. It is said that the top 3 feet of gravel only was shoveled in."[103]

On June 15, 1929 Roshier stumbled across a "small boulder of float quartz with visible gold" [94] just lying there in the creek. In later years, Fred Terrell, a Koyukuk gold miner who had seen the float quartz,

Float quartz with gold[115]

said that he "figured there was $400 worth of gold in that rock."[4] Float quartz is any piece that has fallen away from a pocket of quartz, usually by weathering of a hillside from rain, wind and snow. Sometimes, but not always, the float quartz lies just below the pocket, and if you search the hillside above, you can discover the pocket from which the piece of float quartz fell.

Roshier prospected in the steep hillsides above the creek where he found the piece of float quartz, but he never found the pocket from whence it fell. Roshier hoped to find more quartz pieces with gold in them but never did. Roshier's claim on Surprise Creek reads:

> Notice of location. District of Alaska, Precinct of Koyukuk. Notice is hereby given that the undersigned, having complied with the laws and regulations has located 20 acres (1,320 feet) of placer mining ground situation in Surprise Creek, tributary of the Wild River, Koyukuk Precinct described to wit: Known as Surprise Creek from Discovery Post downstream 1,320 feet to Post No. 2. Northerly direction 660 feet to Post No. 3. Upstream 1,320 feet to Post No. 4 southerly direction 660 feet to Post No. 1. This notice is posted in the No. 1 below discovery of said claim. Discovered June 20, located June 20, 1929. Filed for record by R. H. Creecy, July 23, 1929 at 5 p.m. and recorded in my office. Charles Irish, U.S. Commissioner and Official Recorder.[21]

As recounted in later years during a court proceeding, in August of 1929, Roshier loaned the piece of float quartz to Joe Mathews so that Joe could use it "for the purpose of trying to raise money for supplies for further prospecting." Joe went Outside that fall, taking the float quartz with him, but he failed to raise any money from prospective investors. Upon his return to Alaska, Joe deposited the float quartz with the Alaska Agricultural College and School of Mines in Fairbanks so they could exhibit it. Joe returned to the Wild River country around April 25, 1930. When Roshier learned that Joe had left his prize piece of float quartz at the college instead of bringing back the expected grubstake, he urged Joe to send a note to the

College asking them to deliver it to a roadhouse in Bettles owned by Jay Dodds, who would keep it until Roshier could travel down from the Wild Lake country to collect it. After some delay, Joe finally sent the note, but shortly thereafter he was taken ill and died in the Tanana hospital on October 5, 1933. With Joe's death, the college claimed they did not have proof of who the true owner of the float quartz was and refused to return it to Roshier. Roshier petitioned the court to retrieve his rightful property.

Roshier laid out his case, as a "miner and prospector for gold, both placer and lode" before U. S. Commissioner Charles Irish and waited for his decision.

> On December 2, 1933, the prayer of the petition is hereby granted and it is hereby ordered and decreed that a citation be issued to the Alaska Agricultural College and School of Mines, to show cause why the said large piece of gold-bearing quartz, deposited and left with said school by Joe Mathews not be delivered to Roshier H. Creecy as prayed for in said petition.

The college president, Charles Bunnell, acquiesced to the petition, and on December 29, 1933, he wrote, "Honorable Chas. Irish, U.S. Commissioner, Koyukuk Precinct, Wiseman, Alaska. The item in question will be forwarded to you in such manner as you may direct." On May 3, 1934, nearly five years after discovering the float quartz at Surprise Creek, the court decreed that "said quartz is the property of Roshier H. Creecy."[116]

Fred Terrell recalled that when Roshier got his float quartz back, he took it to Kelly's store in Wiseman for a grubstake. "Kelly turned it over to a whole sale house in Fairbanks for supplies for his store and while it was in Fairbanks they took a chisel to it and chiseled all the gold out of it! There was a big row over it!"[4] In 1933, Roshier sold his claim on Surprise Creek to Volney B. Wakefield.[104]

Around 1930, Roshier began spending more time prospecting in creeks near Wiseman. Later in life, Nathan recalled that when he had mined with his father in the Wild Lake area, Roshier had talked about going over to Kelly's Mistake. "He used to call it the 'lost mine', was about 10 miles south of Wiseman. He was always talking about going there to prospect before I left. I guess he finally did, when Mathews wouldn't hire nobody and they had nothin' to work up there, why he took off and went there, that's all. All alone, what the hell."[49]

Chapter 9

Wiseman

In 1930, a U. S. Census taker found Roshier when he was in Wiseman. Roshier stated that he lived in the Koyukuk and his occupation was miner. His race was Negro. He was head of his household, divorced and had no radio set.[117] Roshier told the census-taker he was not able to read or write —this was, of course, a lie, as he could read and write quite well.

Also in Wiseman in 1930 was Robert "Bob" Marshall (1901–1939), a forester, conservationist, later founder of the Wilderness Society and general observer of people. At the time, Bob was interested in studying tree growth in the Arctic. During the fifteen months that he stayed in Wiseman, he explored the Brooks Range and named the headwaters of the North Fork of the Koyukuk as Gates of the Arctic. The area would later become the Gates of the Arctic National Park and Preserve.

He found the people of Wiseman and their lives so interesting that he decided to stay for a year and conduct a large sociological survey of the people, which he characterized as "the happiest civilization of which I have knowledge." His observations and conversations were published in 1933 in a book entitled *Arctic Village*.[106]

Wiseman, located 60 miles north of the Arctic Circle, arose from a gold mining camp. Beginning in 1904, Nolan Creek, a tributary of Wiseman Creek, was extensively mined for gold. The creek was named for John Nolan, an old Klondiker who made first discovery. To supply Nolan Creek prospectors, Wright's Roadhouse was built at the mouth of Wiseman Creek. By 1908, a town had developed around the roadhouse called Wright City. The post office for Wright City was listed as "Nolan" from 1909 to1923, at which time the community came to be called Wiseman after an early prospector named Peter Weisman.[93, 97, 118] In 1913, Pioneers of Alaska established Wiseman Igloo No. 8, and a Pioneers Hall was built at which community dinners and dances were held. In 1915, an "air of prosperity" was reported in Wiseman— mining was showing good pay and over one hundred people lived there.[95, 118] Two advances greatly improved life in Wiseman. The first was the installation in 1924 of the farthest- north wireless radio station. The second was the building of an airfield, with the first flight to Wiseman occurring on May 5, 1925 when pilot Noel Wien made the trip from Fairbanks in three hours and twenty minutes.[101]

Wiseman was considered an "un-platted mining camp." By 1969, miner Joseph Strunka had secured signatures from over 80 percent of cabin owners to have the town surveyed and platted as an official townsite. He submitted the petition to the Bureau of Land Management, however all Alaskan lands were withdrawn until the Alaska Native Land Claims Settlement Act provisions were implemented. In 1984, Wiseman became a legal townsite, and after cabin owners paid a fee, each received title to their cabin site.[119]

Among the seventy-seven non-native people living in the Koyukuk studied by Bob Marshall was "the Koyukuk's only Negro." Bob described Roshier as a "mulatto Negro who has been in the Arctic for a quarter of a century. It is interesting to note that his [attitude] rating among both white and Eskimos is not very high, though not quite low enough to place him in the most unpopular 20 percent. . . .He is disliked by some, though well-liked by others. He exhibits several of the most unpopular traits which are enough to give anyone in the region a low rating." The "unpopular traits" exhibited by Roshier included telling tall tales of his own heroism, which was frowned upon, and housing his dogs in the government shelter cabins while on the trail, a distinctly unsocial act. Bob goes on to say, "Certainly, he suffers from none of the prejudices which Negroes generally encounter in the U.S. He is welcome in practically everyone's home, has been a partner of many different white men, eats in the roadhouses, stops in the cabins along the trail, and participates in all the social functions just as freely as if he were a white man." Bob found Roshier to be "a most interesting person" and noted how impressed he was with "Rosher Creecy explaining an ingenious experiment he performed on ants."[106] Unfortunately, Bob did not reveal the details of Roshier's experiment.

Although Roshier lacked a formal education, he was well-read and had an active mind. Among the views he shared with Bob was this one: "We say [about the Natives] 'those poor, innocent devils, they don't know enough to develop their resources.' But we come along and squander all our resources 'till we haven't any left! Now, who's the ignorant devils?"[106]

Many of Wiseman's residents were socialists, including Roshier. In fact, Bob Marshall was astounded by the prevalence of socialism in Wiseman. He divided the populace into thirty-seven capitalists, thirty-one socialists and nine malcontents. He recorded an after-dinner conversation of a group of men in his book *Arctic Village*. From Martin Slisco— "It's my belief that they could divide things right today so everybody have everything he need to live. When man hasn't no money, sick, too old, no work to do, everyone else should get together give him money to live. They get it back again anyway." Harry Snowdon— "Yes, Jesus Christ, that's what I can't understand, how some people can be so senseless they don't see that when the poor man's given money it comes right back so everyone benefits by it."[106]

While members of the Wiseman community generally enjoyed content and sociable lives, there was occasional travail, such as food shortages, uncertain mail delivery, injury and accidental death, suicide and crime.

In the early days, **scarcity of food** was a frequent specter. For example, in the April 19, 1912 issue of the *Fairbanks Daily Times* it was reported "On Hammond River, grub of all kinds has been short all winter. No salt, ham, bacon, butter, cream or dried fruit, most live on rabbits and birds." [101] Steamers went up to Bettles but once or twice a year, and from there supplies had to be hand-poled or hauled by horses 80 miles upriver in a scow to Wiseman, costing $140 per ton. By 1915, the advent of gardening by people in Wiseman greatly aided their food security. Potatoes, turnips, cauliflower, carrots and cabbage grew well despite frosts.

Mail delivery was uncertain. In winter, the mail carrier came once a month by dog team, weather permitting. In summer, mail arrived with the infrequent scow from

---

Bettles. Sometimes, no mail left Wiseman for three months or more, especially during break-up.

Injury and accidental deaths were part of bush living. For example, Stanley Ditton got his hand caught in a pump, crushing off a finger. Vern Watts got his hand caught in a circular saw, losing it. W. B. Connell drowned in front of Wiseman when he attempted to swim across the river but cramped. Dick Jones was killed by a methane gas explosion when digging in an old shaft. Many miners froze fingers, toes or feet, requiring amputation. A few miners went off hunting or prospecting by themselves and never returned.[101]

Suicide was not uncommon in the Koyukuk when people became despondent from the harsh and lonely conditions, but everyone in Wiseman was shocked by the suicide of Dr. C. E. Danforth, "a bright and shining man" who had been their physician, U.S. district commissioner, and active Pioneer Lodge member.[101] The May 6, 1919 issue of the *Fairbanks Daily News-Miner* reported, "Dr. Danforth loved the frontier. Took daily walks, visited pioneers. Mined, hunted, cut wood. But camp dwindled to little or nothing. Spirit of camaraderie was gone. It preyed upon his mind. Became nervous. More effort to maintain good spirits. . . Made his will, spread a rubber blanket over his bed, got into his nightgown, folded his clothes on a chair, put the muzzle of his gun over his heart and pulled the trigger."[101]

Crime was rare in Wiseman, but it did happen. There was the case of the hooker who swindled a miner out of his gold poke. The April 23, May 6, November 6, 1913 and February 17, 1914 issues of the *Fairbanks Daily Times* reported the chronicle of Ben Dahl, a miner who struck it rich in Hammond River. Ben developed a "champagne appetite" and gave Norah Moore a poke of gold worth $5,000. When he sobered up, he wanted his poke back. Norah took off with the mail carrier. Ben mushed after them, traveling 45 miles the last day to swear out a warrant for her arrest for stealing. At the trial, Ben stated he had fallen in love with Norah who had promised to marry him so he gave her the gold to sell and set him up in the real estate business in Vancouver. The jury awarded the gold to Norah, leaving Ben with a sad lesson.[101]

Roshier left Wiseman for the Wild Lake area. He was cited in a mining report in the January 26, 1933 *Fairbanks Daily News-Miner*: "Bettles District. Joe Smith and brother F. H. Smith brought four big nuggets found on their Spring Creek ground, 60 miles north of Bettles . . . R. H. Creecy has put down a couple of holes and has found good pay. Smith says the country is a good one for anyone who wants to take a chance."[101]

The following year, Roshier's explorations took him north and east of Wiseman. In Reed's mineral survey of the upper Koyukuk region, he noted that work was conducted on Jim Pup Creek (also called Jim Gulch) by "Creecy, Pat Kelleher, and Hans Christensen." Jim Pup Creek is a 2.5 mile-long eastern tributary of California Creek, by Big Lake. Gold was discovered on Jim Pup Creek in 1901. The gold was coarse and the pay streak was said to be 10 feet wide, overlain with only 3–5 feet of gravel.[103, 120] Thereafter, Roshier prospected in a small tributary to the Middle Fork of the Koyukuk called Gold Creek, where he staked a claim. Placer gold had been discovered on Gold Creek as early as 1900, but "production fell off rapidly after 1905."[120] Gold Creek was reported to have produced $232,000 in gold by 1909.[121]

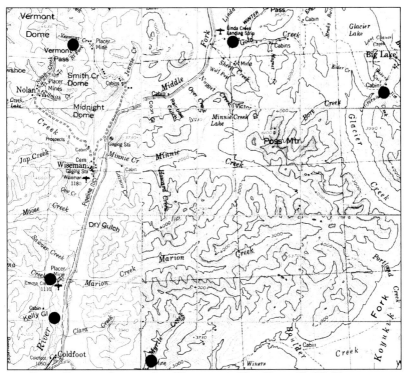

Dots denote the creeks (Vermont, Jim Pup, Gold, Emma, Kelly's Mistake, Myrtle) where Roshier Creecy was known to have mined for gold in the Wiseman area, 1917–1948[105]

A U.S. Geological Survey report on the mineral industry in Alaska in 1934 listed active miners in the northern part of the Koyukuk Mining District:

On Archibald Creek, a tributary of Nolan Creek, Peter Dow and Oliver Chappell; on the lower part of Nolan Creek, John Wooll (two camps), Peter Haslem and associates, Charles LeBoyteau, Sam Standish, Oliver Chappell, and Joe Ulen; on Smith Creek, the drift mines of Bobby Jones, Sam White and O'Leary and Smith Wanamaker, Jess Allen and George Eaton, open cuts of

127

Smith Wanamaker and Hugh Boyle; on Hammond River, the drift mines of Michael Anglich, James Kelly, Harry Foley and Bill Burke, Thomas Brady, Vern Watts, Kenneth Harvey and Victor Neck, and Ike Spinks and Charles Irish and the summer prospecting on the bench on the west side of the creek by Ernest Collins; on Union Creek, the open cut of Vern Watts; on Sheep Creek, the drift mine of Frank Miller and associates; on Gold Creek, the summer work of Roshier Creecy and of Patrick Kelleher; on Jim Pup, in the Big Lake area, the drift mine of Hans Christenson; on Lake Creek, the drift mine of George Mangles and John Rooney; on Mascot Creek the open cut of Vincent Knorr; on Porcupine Creek, the drift mine of Samuel and Oberin Standish and the open-cut mine of Victor Neck; on Clara Creek, the open-cut mine of Kenneth Harvey; on Myrtle Creek the open-cut mines of Peter Haslem and associates and William Marr.[122]

Roshier's cabin on Gold Creek[123]

Roshier was alone on Gold Creek except for an old Irishman, Patrick J. Kelleher (1861–1935), who had been with him on Jim Pup Creek. In 1934, a prospector named Harry B. Leonard (1899–1989) moved in downstream. In a 1978 interview, Harry explained: "I first run into Creecy when I first came to the country. He was on Gold Creek." Harry said that he and some fellas flew to Big Lake, then floated on a raft down the Bettles River to the Middle Fork of the Koyukuk River and passed by Gold Creek, aiming to land in Wiseman. Harry launched into a narrative:

We had landed over there by Bettles River. We built a raft way up there out of some old cabin logs and come down and tied off of Gold Creek over there. That's when I first met Creecy, 4th of July. Did I tell you about the first time I seen him over there shoveling at Gold Creek? I tied the raft and walked on over there and Creecy was shoveling in there and he took a pan to show us the gold. Pretty good pan there, you know, probably 15–20 cents. "Oh!" he says "this is no good!" and threw the pan as far as he could throw it!" [Laughter] "Now come with me" he says, "I'll show you somethin'!" The creek where he was working there. . . he'd cut into the bedrock 10 or 12 feet on each side and the water was low. We walked up the creek in back of him and every once in awhile I'd see a little color of gold down close in the water and I'd pick it up, see, and we got up there a ways, I guess I musta picked up three or four nuggets. Then Creecy says, "Now we'll go back down, I'll show you!" We started back down there and Creecy stopped and looked and looked.

"That's funny" he says "Along here I saw color here yesterday!" I never told Creecy I picked up those nuggets. [Laughter] He put 'em there, you know! Stuck 'em in the edge of the bedrock!

I told him I'm goin' down to Wiseman. Creecy decided he was going along. He said, "You fellas, you don't know . . . I've rafted every river in this country!" And he talked about rafting down river and the troubles he had along the way. Says, "I'll show you how to raft!" He had a pretty good-sized raft, too. Pinned the raft logs. Pretty close to the mouth of the [Middle Fork of the Koyukuk] River, when it comes into the Koyukuk River, kind of a canyon there, before you get to the mouth of it, right at the start of the canyon, why, the river's cut back under quite a ways—it's limestone there. And Creecy, he was up at the front of the raft and he was supposed to be guiding the raft, you know. I see the raft is headed right to the bluff, and Creecy, he just stood there and we went right up against that bluff there and it went on an angle where it hit that bluff and one side [of the raft] went down and Creecy was in the front, shouting "Shove it off! Shove it off!" [Laughter] Standing there in the water up to his waist! I had a long pole but it couldn't even touch the bottom! [Laughter] Finally got off the bluff and come on down the river, right in the middle of the river, there was an island, come around one side of that island there, and when we come to where the other branch of the river come in that god-damned raft went straight down! We finally come up there and my old dog had been on there and I looked up and he never come up. He finally came up and went over to the bank. We come down and tied that raft right in front of the [Slisco] roadhouse, that's where the [Koyukuk] river was back then.[5]

After their rafting adventure, Roshier and Harry became friends. "I stayed on Gold Creek. Creecy stayed there a couple years. Creecy'd been on every creek in this country, all over. He never got rich. To be a good miner, you had to be lucky and find a lot of gold."[5] The two men never mined together. "Creecy always went by himself, except when he had his boy with him over at Wild Lake," Harry said, but the two men visited one another. Harry had many anecdotes to relate about Roshier and said he had a hard time telling truth from fiction. "He liked to tell stories, but I had to sort the straight from the bull. Creecy was witty all right. He wanted you to analyze them stories. He'd say, 'Analyze that!' Some of them stories, that's a lot of bull shit. You were supposed to analyze what part was straight and what wasn't."[5]

Several of Roshier's stories were about food, of keen interest to prospectors who hunted and gathered most of their food, with the purchase of a few store-bought staples. A January 1930 grocery receipt from Sam Dubin, who owned stores in Bettles, Wiseman, Alatna and Fairbanks, was found among Roshier's effects after his death and provides an idea of what the local trading post had to offer.

Roshier bought supplies on several dates in January at the Bettles store, which suggests he was staying for a few weeks at his cabin in Old Bettles, stocking up before heading back into the hills for the rest of the winter. The supplies included fish (probably for his dogs), crackers, potatoes, two dozen eggs, bacon, Hills coffee, Campbell soup, lard, yellow corn-meal, apples, dried figs, candles, moccasins, overalls, and two shovels.

First page of a January 1930 grocery receipt found among Roshier's effects after his death[21]

There were times when Roshier had nothing to eat. One incident occurred at Chandalar Lake where Roshier ran out of food. At the outlet of the creek he saw a fin of a fish. He grabbed it by the gills. The fish was so big it dragged him to the middle of the lake and he had to let go. Roshier told Harry, "Sometimes when I run out of meat, I'll go settle down into the 'nigger heads' [Tundra tussocks] and wait for a little mouse to come up between the clumps of grass, then hit it over the head and eat it. Once, I found an eagle's nest, and when the adult came back to the nest with food for the young, I made so much noise below the tree that the startled eagle dropped its prey, giving me another easy meal." At times, when he ran out of food, common sense overcame his desire to be independent and he sought other miners or natives who had provisions they could spare. Once, when he was out of food, Roshier built a raft and floated downriver to Wiseman. Relatives of Sammy Hope's picked him up and fed him for a couple of weeks. Roshier also told Harry about times when meat was plentiful. During one month in the fall the "refrigerator" had one sheep, two caribou and one moose. In the summer he caught salmon, whitefish and grayling in the nearby creeks and rivers. He also bought bales of dried salmon (12–14 fish each) from the Athabascan people for his dogs. Roshier picked blueberries and cranberries in late summer which were frozen and a good source of vitamin C for the winter. He supplemented his wild diet with store food. Like fellow miners, Roshier was adept at making hardtack. For water, "You go to get a pile of snow, melt it on the stove, come back and find at the bottom of the pot there'd be rabbit pellets sittin' there! Have to start over!"[5]

Harry said that Roshier liked to fool people, play jokes on them, or get the upper hand. Roshier hunted every fall for moose and caribou as a supply of meat for the winter. One year, he went with another miner to Boulder Creek to hunt. "There was some fellas over at Big Lake, one of these fellas and him wanted to go huntin' to Boulder Creek. This fella, he counted out everything for how many days they'd be gone, what they'd eat for each meal. So they started out and stopped for lunch in the middle of the day and this fella was makin' tea. He says to Creecy, 'Creecy, how many shall I put in?' It was concentrated tea in pellets, it looked like caribou droppings. Creecy said 'Put 'em all in!' The tea was extra strong that night, and the entire trip's tea supply was gone! He'd tell stories like that."[5] Harry laughed as he told another story about Roshier.

A miner named Roy was out hunting and ran into Creecy, who told him he had just seen two caribou go over the side of the nearby hill. Roy went over the hill and never found the caribou, came back and confronted Creecy. Roy asked Creecy why he had lied like that and Creecy replied that it was just the "nigger" in him!

Creecy stayed on Gold Creek a couple years, I used to go up and visit him, there was nobody else there, rapped on his door, come in, he was laying on his bed sick, moaning and groaning. "Creecy, you're pretty sick, I'll go get my dogs and take you to town." He said, "No sir, I'll die right here." It was after Christmas, somebody had sent me a bottle of this Hudson Bay rum and I'd told Creecy about it before. "I'll go get that bottle of rum I have and bring it back and make you a hot drink." I brought it back, mixed him a few drinks, he got over his moanin' and groanin' anyway! I stayed there a little while and I says, "Creecy, I'm goin' home but I'll leave this bottle here and tonight you can mix you up a hot drink." I came back the next morning and the bottle was half empty and he was all right! He got away with half a bottle of my rum![5]

During the 1930s, Roshier applied and was accepted into membership of the Pioneers of Alaska, Igloo No. 8.[59] The Pioneers in Wiseman sought to promote social interactions and provide help when needed, such as food and medical care. His application was endorsed by his neighbor on Gold Creek, Patrick J. Kelleher, and by George Huey (1855–1936), U.S. district commissioner in Wiseman in 1924–1925. Both men stated they had known Roshier for ten years and verified that "He is a man of good moral character and we verily believe all his statements are true."[59]

Roshier Creecy panning for gold in winter, circa 1930s[123]

On his application, Roshier stated he had been born in Virginia on January 10, 1871 (a birth year four years later than his sister's recollection and five years later than early U.S. census data). He first came to Skagway in January 1897 and arrived in Wiseman in 1911. Roshier gave as his home address the home of his sister, Mrs. Virginia McIver in McDonald, West Virginia. For identification purposes, he stated he was 5 feet 8 inches tall, weighed 170 pounds, his eyes were colored brownish-gray, his hair color was sandy, his complexion was dark and he had a medium forehead. Roshier must have had a chuckle with himself when his application was accepted because the initial membership requirements to join Pioneers of Alaska were "white men who came to Alaska before January 1, 1900."[124] But, the Pioneers in Wiseman who sponsored Roshier didn't care about color; Roshier was one of them.

Roshier takes turns with his dogs pulling a sled of supplies, circa 1930s[123]

At the end of the winter of 1935, Harry was on Gold Creek and he recalled going on a trip with Roshier. "Old Pat Kelleher, he had Discovery claim on Gold Creek, he was about ready to die, I guess, old Pat got something wrong with him. Creecy had these two dogs, Creecy was takin' Pat [in his sled] to town [Wiseman] and I was along, too. We got about, oh half way between Gold Creek and Hammond River and there was bunch of three or four little gulches that come in there, you know? Creecy was askin' Pat what the name of these gulches was 'Pat, what's the name of that gulch?' I don't know whether it was the first gulch or the second one, I was a little ways in back of 'em snowshoeing and ol' Pat says, 'That's Coon Creek!' and Creecy turned around. [Laughter] That's the name of that gulch!"[5] Roshier lost his friend, Pat Kelleher, who died in Wiseman shortly after their arrival, on April 22, 1935.

Harry said that in addition to placer mining, Roshier did some hardrock mining. "Creecy would be talkin' about mining and he would say, 'I likes to dig!'" Harry saw Roshier dig trenches 15 to 20 feet deep, looking for a rich gold vein. While Roshier used a wood fire to thaw the ground, Harry mostly used an upright boiler, rather than a wood fire. "Creecy got a little gold, panning and sluicing, a little grubstake, but that pension, $30 a month was good money." Harry noted that geologists with the U.S. Geological Survey would come around to the mining camps and talk to the miners. Roshier once told Harry about his encounter with a geologist named J. B. Mertie. "He was over on a creek Creecy was working. He come up on this creek and Creecy says, 'Mr. Mertie, how deep is it to bedrock here?' Mertie looked at him and says, 'You've been here longer than I have, you ought to know!' Creecy says, 'That's what I call a smart man.'"[5]

Harry was asked to describe Roshier. "Creecy wasn't real dark. In fact, Charlie Breck told me he thought Creecy was an Eskimo when he first met him. Creecy never talked about feeling discriminated against because of his race. He had a little of an accent, like black people talk, but not much. Was he well-educated? No, but he wasn't ignorant. He could read and write. He never talked about going back Outside. He didn't have any girlfriends that I ever knew of."[5]

Friends Harry Leonard (left) and Roshier Creecy (right), near Gold Creek, circa 1930s[123]

Roshier's time on Gold Creek fell into the usual rhythm of bush life, as recorded in scraps of notes he kept. Visitors were rare and worth a special notation: "Return from hunting October 2, cold at knight. Commence hauling meat October 17th. Return November 20th with frozen feet. December 12th Sammy Hope arrived from town." Although he only went to Wiseman a few times a year, he enjoyed seeing a special friend there named Tishu Ulen. Tishu was an Inupiaq native born in 1905 near Chandalar Lake. She was named after her grandmother Anna Tishu. She first met Roshier when she was a little girl living in Old Bettles. "Everybody called him Rosy or Roshier. He had a cabin in Old Bettles. In the winter time he'd go back and forth, between Bettles and his cabins at Rye Creek."[98] In a 1981 interview, Tishu recounted a few memories of her life in Bettles around 1917–1919. She would save up her money, and when the sternwheeler *Reliance* came to town, she would go down to the dock and buy apples, oranges and lemons "for $3, it was a real treat."[98] Later in life, she married Elmer "Joe" Ulen and they moved to Wiseman.

Roshier Creecy at his cabin, circa 1930s[123]

Of Roshier, Tishu said, "He didn't drink much, he smoked. He had good teeth. He's not too dark, mulatto. He was a good-sized man. He was friendly. He had two dogs, fat, he kept them well fed. He had a sled. He went all over that country. Creecy would come and go from his cabin, not stay [in Wiseman] all winter. When he came to town, he would spend a few nights at Martin Slisco's roadhouse or with Big Jim Suckik. Big Jim was from Unalakleet. Then he would be away again. He was good to us. Us kids would come to Big Jim's house and he always had paper and pencil and write. He read to us." In fact, Roshier helped teach Tishu how to write. She explained that Roshier prospected by himself and didn't make a lot of money at it. "He never worked for wages—he had that pension."[98]

The residents of Wiseman enjoyed having community dinners and social dances at the Pioneer's Hall using a "great big old Victrola and a stack of records." Everyone was welcome to join in. They especially had a big party at Christmas. Tishu said that Roshier never came in for the dances or Christmas parties. "He never come. I saw him dance, though. My mother had the store there and she had some music on the radio and he walked in the door and started dancing. He was really kicking his heels up!"[98]

Several of the old prospectors around Wiseman had a few things to say about Roshier. Charlie Breck (1916–1992) had a cabin in Wiseman. In an interview in 1978, Charlie remembered a story about Roshier "Something Oliver L. Chappell (1897–1981) mentioned to me." [Chappell mined on Archibald Creek and was a U.S. postmaster at Wiseman.] "Oliver, he was from Alabama, he once asked Creecy how he was doing, and Creecy said, 'Oh fine, I've got three white men workin' for me!' [Laughter] I met him a couple of times. He was all over. I just went up to Wiseman a couple times during the winter, to pick up mail." Charlie said he stuck pretty close to his place, similar to Creecy. "Several of the old miners, they stayed to themselves, didn't come to town much."[6]

Then there was Fred Terrell (1908–1985) who came to Wiseman in 1936 from Juneau and mined on Bettles River. When Fred came to Wiseman, the population was about 125 people. Fred was a U.S. postmaster at Wiseman for a few years. In a 1978 interview, Fred recalled Roshier. "Creecy was all over. He was a good entertainer. When Creecy came to town, he had the floor. He was a pretty good talker." Fred was told a story about Roshier by his friend, Gustaf "Gus" S. Larson, a Swede who mined around Bettles River.

Gus was askin' Creecy about something and Creecy gave him a big line. And Gus says, "Creecy you know you're the biggest liar in this country!" Creecy says, "I know it, I admit it, but your own tongue will lie to you. I'll give you an example. Got to feelin' around in my mouth with my tongue and felt a cavity in my tooth. It felt so big you could stick the end of a pick handle in it. I went to the cabin and got a mirror and had to have a magnifyin' glass just to see it. Your own tongue'll lie to you!"[4]

I remember another story I heard him tellin' before my time up there. They were freighting with dogs for this [Northern Commercial Company] store in Wiseman, four or five teams of 'em, and they got down to Bettles and got in a snow storm and everybody waitin' for the other to break the trail. So, Creecy, he hooked up his dogs and lugged his stuff and took off first, breaking trail, and he went to the first dry patch of woods, set up his tent and got in his sleeping bag and said he had a pile of magazines and started readin'. So, the other drivers all hooked up their dogs and set out to follow the broken trail, but didn't go very far before they found Creecy in a tent readin' a magazine! One or two of 'em went on to break the rest of the trail.[4]

When asked to describe Roshier, Fred said,

He had curly hair and he was light and had blue eyes. He could pass for a Caucasian. He was about 180 pounds, he was a pretty well-built man. He got a pension from the army, that's the way he got by in that country. I was never around him much. I'd run into him in Wiseman. Maybe wouldn't see him for a year or so. Creecy was on Gold Creek at that time and Harry Leonard was on Gold Creek, below Creecy. Creecy was a loner. He'd come to town a few times in the winter. He'd not tell people if he found anything or not, he'd tell a big story. He'd say "I dug a big hole, there wasn't any gold in it, but it was the finest diggin' you ever saw!" Creecy, nobody ever knew what he did, how many ounces of gold he took out. Kept a pretty closed mouth about that. He'd take off in the winter with dogs and sled and a tent. He was kind of radical, political, mostly on Jim Crow stuff. For instance, white people over the colored race, back before we had desegregation, he'd get strung out on it, say, "American people are pretty cruel!" something of that order.[4]

Fred was asked if there was any discrimination toward Roshier. "Oh no, everybody liked Creecy, he got along with everybody. He'd just give you a Creecy story. He was strictly a loner. He come to my area, dig a hole within half a mile of me and never come near me. He used wood fires in winter for prospecting. Dig about three holes at once, make a fire in there at night and cover it with black rock, sheet iron, bank it. Get up in the morning and dig it out. Sometimes you get as much as a foot, but with mud, you'd get 3–4 inches."[4]

In 1935, Roshier's notes indicate he was ill. "August 1st 1935 leave Wiseman for Fairbanks very sick." Upon arriving in Fairbanks, a reporter with the *Fairbanks Daily News-Miner* interviewed him on August 8 when it became known that he had not left the Koyukuk for the past thirty years: "R. H. Creecy flew from Wiseman to Fairbanks for medical attention. Last visited Fairbanks in 1906 just before going to the Koyukuk. Fascinated by autos, calling them 'porcupines' as he doesn't know which end is the front." Doctors in Fairbanks sent him to Seattle for surgery. Roshier did not return to Wiseman for nearly eight months. During his absence from Alaska, his condition was monitored by friends who gave periodic updates to the *Fairbanks Daily News-Miner.* "Roshier Creecy of Wiseman underwent second stage of a major operation this morning and doing as well as can be expected . . . Roshier Creecy convalescing well . . . Roshier Creecy of Wiseman now permitted to leave bed . . . Roshier Creecy will leave hospital within next day or two."[101]

The November 25, 1935 issue of the *Fairbanks Daily News-Miner* ran an article: "Roshier H. Creecy coming back in March. Won't spend another 30 years north of the Arctic Circle! Lived in upper Koyukuk for nearly 30 continuous years. Four months ago, he saw his first auto, ate his first fresh fruit in 30 years. Shocked by women's modern dress." Roshier sent a clipping of the article to his sister, Virginia. Years later, Virginia's granddaughter, Loma R. Pointer of Detroit, Michigan, recalled in a 1978 interview that Roshier would send Virginia "little nuggets of gold, and she would send him peppermint candy. My grandma had a little store in Beckley, West Virginia. When I visited my grandma, I was tasked with addressing the envelopes to uncle Roshier in Alaska."[2]

Roshier did go back to the Arctic and he never left Alaska again. An old stampeder wrote, "You don't know it's got hold of you while you're up here, but before you've been Outside a month, all at once you find it pulling at you, it never lets up. . . Maybe there ain't a darn soul up here you care about! Maybe you ain't got an interest in a claim worth hen's teeth! Maybe you're broke and know you'll have to work like a go-devil when you get here! It don't make any difference. It's just Alaska. It calls you and calls you."[61]

Following his return to Alaska, Roshier wrote several letters. He wrote to Louis Dale "L.D." Colbert (1876–1947), a miner and aspiring politician who was a founding director of the Alaska Chapter of the American Mining Congress formed in Fairbanks in 1919. Roshier needed a placer power of attorney from L.D. to hold a mining claim for him, which L.D. sent to Roshier in a letter dated March 6, 1936. Federal mining law stated that in Alaska, any agent could locate and hold a mining claim for another person if the agent obtained a power of attorney from said person. In other states, the power of attorney did not have to be in writing. However, for Alaska, the power of attorney must be in writing, signed, acknowledged, witnessed and recorded. Apparently, this law was considered a pain in the butt by Roshier and L.D. In their correspondence, the two men exchanged political views about President Roosevelt's response to the Great Depression.

Dear Creecy,

Enclosed is Power of Attorney, it must be recorded in the staking district to be any good. I shall certainly stand to knock the Power of Attorney at this election. This present law is not good as the federal law, and should be repealed, but $100 assessment annually on each 20 acres should be retained. . .

You are right about all this government spending it's got to be paid for. I think it is being stopped now, the popular demand against it was too great, but that is only for election purposes, if Roosevelt is re-elected as you think he will, consider it a mandate to go ahead and spend more than ever on socialistic schemes like the Matanuska Colony.

That the Roosevelt Policies, the New Deal, has failed is clear to everyone now. I think he must fall with them. He now has a large support but as it becomes clearer, that the New Deal is impractical, down he must go, like other popular idols. This country works fast.

As for Alaska politics, Diamond is not popular. I think Hurley will be elected Senator and Nerland in the House. I shall stand for more airplane landing fields, return to Federal Placer Act, knock out pwr of atty but retain $100 assess on 20 acres, raise old timer pensions- no paupers oath, and Federal money spent on miners not farmers.

Best Regards, L.D. Colbert. Fairbanks.[21]

The Great Depression gripped the nation beginning in 1929 and lasted ten years. While the New York stock market crash was largely to blame for the onslaught of unemployment, homelessness, hunger and displacement, other contributing factors included: low prices for agricultural goods forced farmers off their land; high tariffs stifled trade; low worker wages meant less money spent and in circulation; thousands of banks failed with a loss of savings for millions of people. President Herbert Hoover believed the economy would recover without government intervention; his policies failed. When Franklin D. Roosevelt was elected president in 1932, he initiated a program called the **New Deal**. The program had three purposes: give relief to the needy; provide jobs; reform laws governing business and government to prevent another depression of such a magnitude. The U.S. government spent money it didn't have (deficit spending) on relief programs and providing jobs to build roads, bridges, dams, etc. Currency began to circulate again, tariffs were lowered so trade improved, and the country slowly recovered. Alaska was the recipient of a New Deal solution to help Midwest farmers recover from bankruptcy. Selected farmers were given loans to farm 40 acres in the Matanuska Valley, located in southcentral Alaska. The farm families were transported by train to Seattle, then loaded onto army transport ships bound for Seward. The farmers found wilderness, requiring extensive clearing. Many left, but those who remained came to be called the **Matanuska Colony**, one of several rural rehabilitation colonies established around the country during the Great Depression.[125, 126]

Roshier also wrote a letter to Walter Johnson, national commander of the Regular Veterans Association (RVA) in Washington, D.C. When Roshier was hospitalized, the Veterans Bureau reduced his pension in half, to just $15. Nationwide, men who served in the military prior to the Spanish-American War were seeing their pensions systematically reduced by the Veterans Bureau, so Roshier's experience was not an isolated incident and the issue was receiving much attention. In protest, Roshier turned to the RVA for assistance. Roshier received a response to his letter, dated March 30, 1936, from Johnson. In his letter to Roshier, Johnson highlighted the battle for power between two branches of the federal government: Congress (which established the pension) and the executive branch (which ordered the pension reduction). Johnson argued that the Executive branch had no authority to repeal acts of Congress. The struggle between the branches of government in 1936 echo today's headlines.

Dear Comrade,

I have your letter wherein you state that you are entitled to $30 a month for total disability incurred in the service prior to the war with Spain, and that the Veterans Bureau reduces your pension to $15 per month while you are being hospitalized.

The rate of $30 per month for total disability incurred in the service in the line of duty was established by the Act of March 3, 1883. You are being pensioned under a rate which was established according to the standards of more than half a century ago and which was probably based on the living standards and wages then prevailing. It is hoped and expected that before many weeks elapse that a change will be made in pension rates.

It is my opinion that you are being illegally and unjustly reduced in pension. . . It is not conceivable for the Executive Power to take away something granted by Congress, or, in other words, for the Executive branch of the government to repeal Acts of Congress.

We know that the Veterans Bureau is reducing pensions of pre-Spanish War men and it is hoped that we will be able to take them to Court. . . Our entire time is taken with pushing for legislative changes which will recognize that the Regular Service Man is an American, too, and provide more reasonable and just pensions for them.

With best personal regards, I am yours in Comradeship, Walter Johnson[21]

One can argue that since Roshier had been tramping about northern Alaska prospecting for gold during the past thirty years, his claim of total disability was questionable on some level. Nonetheless, Roshier had been granted a pension, and he was determined to receive it!

Chapter 10

Troubling Times

On November 18, 1936, Roshier decided to make a trip from his cabin on Gold Creek to Wiseman to buy supplies. It was −52°F. He had spent many years traveling on northern rivers in winter and knew to watch for overflow. But on this trip he was either careless or unlucky, because he froze his feet. By the time he got to Wiseman, he was in bad shape. Thankfully, the town had gained a new resident in the fall of 1934 named George B. Rayburn (1903–1993) who had medical training. Before coming to Wiseman, George was employed as a nurse at Saint Joseph's Hospital in Fairbanks while he was going to school at the Alaska Agricultural College and School of Mines. In a 1980 interview, George explained: "I graduated in 1933. We had a patient from Wiseman by the name of Carl Gustaf Frank who was in for surgery. He was an old man and long-time resident of the Koyukuk." Carl questioned George about his ability to teach school. George, who had received a minor in education, said he was qualified. After Carl returned to Wiseman, he asked the commissioner of education in Juneau, Anthony Karns, to send George an application for a teaching position. George applied, was accepted and given a contract. In early September of 1934, Noel Wien flew George to Wiseman in a Stinson

Gullwing Reliant airplane. The one-room school house had from five to thirteen students in grades 1 through 8.[127, 128]

George recalled, "It was during my stay in Wiseman that I met Roshier Creecy, a black man, and the only black man in the Koyukuk that I know of. It was apparent that I had been hired because I had knowledge of first aid and could be of assistance in medical needs. Roshier was coming to town from Gold Creek, where he mined. He was walking, there was overflow but he didn't know it, and he got his feet wet and it was cold enough that his feet froze before he got to town. I communicated with Dr. Gillespie with the Fairbanks Clinic and he told me treatment should be one of skill-full neglect, where I kept sterile Vaseline gauze dressings on the feet, especially the toes, for some months. This healing process took a long time. It didn't smell very good either—it was a decay of the flesh and subsequent removal. As the flesh became loose, the bandage itself would pull it off. I don't really think it was very painful because that part of the foot was pretty well gone—the toes. I think the end result was that he came into Fairbanks after a period of about five months and they did some minor surgery and sewed the skin back over the stumps of the bones and I believe at that time he was pronounced cured. All I did was dress the feet and apparently that's all the doctors would have done had he come to Fairbanks."[127, 128]

George described his impressions of Roshier. "I got acquainted with him and found him very likeable and a fine man. He was about 5 feet 9 inches tall, muscular. If you're mining, you're getting plenty of exercise. He had a fairly dark complexion, but not completely black. I'm trying to think if there was any discrimination against him because of his color

150

and I can think of none. I believe he was fully accepted in the community as anyone else. He did mine by himself and that was no particular thing, other men did the same thing. It was more common for two or three men to get together, but there were a number of instances of single men working claims by themselves. He may have been depressed to some extent [about his frozen feet], but I recall no complaints. He was, I thought, very objective about it, had accepted the fact that it had happened and would have to get along with it and do the best he could and that was a common attitude up there. Jess Allen lost his hand and wrist while mining and there was no talk about it. Just one of those things that happened and you have to accept it and do the best you can. To help him get around, Roshier had a good stick that he used, carved from willow. He was not a difficult patient to take care of, he was uncomplaining."[128]

Martin Slisco's Roadhouse in Wiseman[21]

George noted that during his convalescence in Wiseman, Roshier stayed at Martin Slisco's Roadhouse. "I went over there to do the dressing. He was incapacitated for

151

several months." During his recovery, Roshier read a lot, an avid pastime of his. Martin extended credit to anyone who couldn't pay his bill immediately, accepting gold for payment. Roshier paid him back in gold nuggets and eventually settled his account with Martin.

George explained the process of selling gold in Wiseman. Miners took their gold to either Martin Slisco or Billy English at Wiseman Trading Company. "Billy would bag it up and send it to the U.S. Assay Office in Seattle by registered mail and they would assay it, determine how much they were going to pay for it, then either put the money to the credit of Wiseman Trading Company in the miner's account, or, send back the cash. Billy felt that by this method of doing business there would be

Roshier's log of his convalescence in the roadhouse, "71 days board"[21]

no complaints." George related a story of an instance where a miner took his gold to Martin Slisco, who figured what it was worth, gave the miner the money, who later claimed he had been shorted.

For George, one of the most depressing things about living in Wiseman was that bad weather, usually in January, prevented mail delivery for a whole month. The planes were scheduled to come into town twice a month. Noel Wien had taken over the contract, coming in by way of Stevens Village,

Hughes, Alatna and Bettles. Plus, from December 6 to January 6, it was cold and the sun was not above the horizon. "That was depressing. Everybody was glad when they heard the motor of the plane. The boys and girls in school would hear an airplane and their heads would pop up, then school would be let out while the plane was in town."[128] George reminisced about community activities in Wiseman in the early 1930s: "At Christmas, the community gathered at the Pioneers Hall. The children would do a play or recitation, there was a dance afterwards with music from a hand-cranked Victrola. In the main, a very peaceful and harmonious community. There was a trouble maker or two; everybody knew it and made allowances for it, but there were some fine people up there. I don't think that Roshier came into Wiseman often, maybe just three or four times a year and that would be about it."[127, 128]

As George mentioned, Roshier was an avid reader, and he subscribed to a large variety of publications including the following found among his effects after his death.[21] A foray into Roshier's reading material opens a window into his thoughts and opinions on the pressing issues of his time.

- **The Progressive.** A monthly liberal magazine founded in 1909 in Wisconsin, focused on politics, culture and progressivism. Articles championed civil rights and liberties, labor rights, immigrant rights, women's rights and pacifism. The magazine condemned racial segregation.

- **The Literary Digest.** A weekly magazine published from 1890 to 1938 in New York City. Focused on opinion pieces, news analysis, and condensation of articles. Roshier saved an article with the startling title, "Should America have a federal anti-lynching law?"

Should America have a federal anti-lynching law?

Pro

PUBLIC OPINION in the United States will never be satisfied until Judge Lynch has received his death sentence. I am sure that the cause of enacting a federal law will enlist right-thinking people until they form an unconquerable army. —*Senator Robert F. Wagner (New York).*

Congress has brought labor relations under federal law, and if it can go to that extreme with the approval of the Supreme Court it can pass a law for the enforcement of provisions of the Constitution as stated in the fourteenth amendment. A federal anti-lynching law will apply everywhere in the United States and cannot be regarded as directed at a particular section of the country—*Chicago Tribune.*

The passage of the anti-lynch bill is vital to the fight for the constitutional rights of the Negro people in America. Let all those who believe in democracy and who hate the barbarous crime of lynching say to the Senate, with a barrage of telegrams, that the bill must become a law.—*Daily Worker (Communist).*

Such a measure may not stamp out lynching, but we believe that under it fewer night-riders will engage in mob murders and shout, "To hell with law!"—*New York World-Telegram.*

Lynch law is no law. A mob's murder of a Negro, even if he is guilty of the crime with which he is charged, does not cancel the first wrong. It only adds a second. The anti-lynch bill should be enacted.—*St. Louis Post-Dispatch.*

We commend to the attention of every member of Congress the report of the Institute of Public Opinion, which shows that not only the nation as a whole, but the South as a section, *favors* the anti-lynching bill.—*New York Post.*

Lynching must be stopped! If the states cannot stop it, by all means let the federal government step in. Whatever be the truth about states' rights, states really have no right to disregard the rights of citizens.—*The Christian Century.*

One or two federal convictions will do more to stop lynching than all the resolutions passed by all the good-will societies, and all the talk by all the humiliated governors. Lynching is a preventable crime. It will be prevented if the cowards who invariably form the mob know there is a jail waiting at the end of the debauch. —*William Allen White.*

America is disgusted and ashamed of its lynching record. If these atrocities are allowed to continue, the people of this country will not forget that responsibility for them rests on those Congressmen who didn't bother to pass the anti-lynching bill.—*Philadelphia Record.*

SENATOR WAGNER rests his case in favor of the bill

Con

ANYBODY who reads and can understand knows that this law would be unconstitutional. Thank God the Supreme Court is still over there!—*Senator Tom Connally (Texas).*

The major question at issue in the bill is not lynching, but the right of the people to retain control over their local officials. As Senator Bailey has pointed out, a sheriff in North Carolina is responsible to the state and not to the federal government. Should Congress destroy that responsibility, it might seriously impair the American system of local self-government.—*Washington Post.*

Both murderous rape and lynching are most unfortunate, but the jackasses who bray about it in Congress should bear in mind that if there is no crime there will be no lynching. —*Cedartown (Ga.) Standard.*

The bill does not make lynching any more a crime than it has always been. The American Institute of Public Opinion discovered that 72 out of every 100 persons queried favored the bill. But just what was the question which the Institute put before those whom it queried? The question read: "Should Congress pass a law which would make lynching a federal crime?" This phrasing of the question is a misnomer. The crime created by the bill is a failure of sheriffs or other local officials to be duly diligent in preventing and punishing lynchings.—*Mark Sullivan in New York Herald Tribune.*

I tell you that you will not aid the Negro race with this bill, because it is unworkable. The South has reduced the crime of lynching more than 5000 per cent in the last forty years, and that is proof that the tide of public sentiment will take better care of this situation than can any law. —*Representative Hatton W. Sumners (Texas).*

It will take a standing army to enforce a federal anti-lynching law. Such a law will prove very costly to the state. No sheriff will take a chance on handling a prisoner without calling for a National Guard escort, and that means they will have to be ready in barracks all the time.—*Hugh L. White, Governor of Mississippi.*

It is a clear invasion of the rights of the states, the giving 'to the federal government the right of intervention to enforce the criminal laws of a state when the violation is intrastate in character.—*Senator William E. Borah (Idaho).*

The Banner strongly condemns lynching; but it is an offense which should be left to the state courts and state law. The measure before Congress embodies a flagrant and indefensible attempt to usurp the police powers of the states. The bill mobs the federal Constitution.— *Nashville Banner.*

SENATOR CONNALLY submits his disgusted disapproval

Clipping from *The Literary Digest*, December 4, 1937, found among Roshier's effects after his death[21]

Lynchings were predominantly carried out by Caucasians against African Americans in the southern and border states. From 1882 to 1951, about 4,730 people were lynched, of whom the majority (73 percent) were African American.[129] Lynchings were among a slew of efforts by white supremacists to maintain social, economic and political dominance over African Americans because they had lost the Civil War and the option of slave-holding. Other efforts of control by white supremacists were discriminatory voter registration and electoral rules, gerrymandering of voting districts, segregation and Jim Crow laws. Early attempts to pass federal anti-lynching legislation date to 1901 but passage was halted due to filibusters by southern senators. Subsequent anti-lynching bills were introduced in Congress over the last century but all failed to pass due to the powerful southern voting block. The argument made by the southerners was that murder is a state crime, so prosecution should be left to the states. They framed the argument as a states' rights issue. The problem was that law-enforcement officials in the southern states often turned a blind eye to lynching and did not prosecute the perpetrators. The federal bills sought to not only prosecute lynchers if the state failed to do so, but in addition, if authorities did not protect all citizens, they would be punished with fines and jail time.[129, 130] As of this writing (2018) there is still no federal anti-lynching law in the U.S. In spring of 2018, a museum to memorialize lynching was opened in Montgomery, Alabama, called The National Memorial for Peace and Justice. The museum is dedicated to "the victims of American white supremacy" and "demands a reckoning with the lynchings of thousands of black people."[131]

- **The Outlook and Independent.** Two separate periodicals until 1928, when they merged. Published from1893–1935 in New York City, focused on social and political issues. Theodore Roosevelt was an associate editor before being elected the twenty-sixth president of the United States. Another writer of note was Booker T. Washington, an African American educator and author. Roshier saved a section from a July 9, 1930 issue of this magazine entitled "Prosperity and Prohibition" in which the author argued for repeal of the Eighteenth Amendment. "Then at least the government would receive in taxes the millions that now go to bootleggers and so to finance the most powerful and dangerous underworld this country has ever known."

- **The Chicago Defender.** A weekly newspaper founded in 1905 in Chicago for primarily African American readers and continues to be in circulation. The newspaper reported on and campaigned against Jim Crow era violence, racial segregation, and southern lynchings. It played a large role in urging southern African Americans to migrate to the northern states.

- **The Pittsburgh Courier.** A weekly newspaper published 1907 to1966 in Pittsburgh for African American readers. The newspaper vowed to "abolish every vestige of Jim Crowism" in Pittsburgh. It focused on social progress by covering injustice and advocating for improvements in housing, education and employment. The newspaper also ran serialized novels and highlighted sports in the African American Leagues. An annual subscription cost $4.00 in 1943.

- *Negro Digest.* A monthly magazine published in Chicago from 1942 to 1951, returned in 1961, renamed *Black World*, and published to 1976 for the African American audience. Focused on positive stories about the African American community.

- *Soviet Russia Today.* A monthly magazine published from 1932 to 1951 in New York by Friends of the Soviet Union, part of the Communist Party. Focused on Soviet politics and conditions in Soviet Russia.

- *Congressional Record—Appendix.* First published in 1873, it is the official publication of debates and proceedings of the U.S. Congress. The Appendix, or "Statements for the Record," includes speeches, letters or testimony not given in person. It was made available to the public beginning in 1875. Roshier kept several sections relating to the New Deal, an argument for America to stay out of foreign wars, and a bill prepared by the American Indian Federation objecting to policies toward native people by the Bureau of Indian Affairs. Roshier likely saw parallels between how the U.S. government treated Native Americans and African Americans.

- *Seward Weekly Gateway.* Published from 1905 to1914, in Seward, Alaska, it focused on Alaskan news. Roshier kept a May 9, 1933 clipping about an Alaskan law approving and regulating the sale of beer and wine. The repeal of Prohibition was not fully ratified until December 5, 1933, but Alaskan legislators were not wasting a second.

- *Fairbanks Daily News-Miner.* Founded in 1904, the Fairbanks newspaper was published under several names and continues to be in circulation. It focuses on local and Alaskan news.

- ***The American Veteran.*** A monthly magazine founded in 1931 and printed in Washington, D.C. Devoted to disseminating facts of interest to veterans including legislation, court decisions, opinion pieces, veteran viewpoints, advice.

March 1936 *The American Veteran* magazine, illustrating the problems facing veterans—burning of homeless veteran camps and reduction of pensions by passage of the Economy Act [21]

By spring of 1937, Roshier had recovered from his injury and resumed life in his cabin on Gold Creek. According to 1937 issues of the *Fairbanks Daily News-Miner* Wiseman was populated at this time with "48 houses and 127 whites and Eskimos." Martin Slisco's roadhouse and trading post welcomed all, providing homemade meals for $1.50, hosting phonograph dances, moving pictures and a radio that brought the news. James Kelly and Billy English ran two other trading stores in Wiseman. There were sixteen children in the town. Oldtimers worked the creeks with thirty-nine open-cut mines; fifteen operated with shaft and drift methods. "Nuggets weighing as high as 60 or 70 ounces are frequently found, but they are not too numerous and pay is spotty. No big machinery yet in the upper Koyukuk Valley, small operators use mining methods of the early days."[101]

Roshier's notes relate the arrival of spring and with it the break-up of creeks and rivers: "Robins arrive on the creek May 10th 1937. Gold Creek May 23rd 1937 open up at 11:30 a.m. from rim to rim with a slide. Drowned out cabin, full of water." He continued to wander all over the upper Koyukuk prospecting new sites ("Leave Wiseman for Emma Creek February 23, 1937"); working old claims ("Leave Wiseman for Gold Creek, supper, no breakfast March 4, 1937"); and re-visiting Bettles ("Leave Bettles for Wiseman October 23rd 1938. Arrive on Gold Creek November 1st 1938")—all despite losing portions of his feet to frostbite.

Geologist Irving Reed reported in his 1937 mineral reconnaissance of the upper Koyukuk region that there were three operations mining on Gold Creek: Charles and Jack Horner were on claim no. 11, R. H. Creecy was on claim no. 8, and Harry Leonard was on claim no. 2 above Discovery. Reed also recorded in 1937 that R. H. Creecy had started an open cut on Kelly's Mistake Creek.[103] Kelly's Mistake Creek, also called Kelly's Gulch, is a steep western tributary of the Middle Fork of the Koyukuk River, 2 miles south of Emma Creek. The creek got its name when James Kelly (1877–1944) started prospecting there, all the time thinking he was on Emma Creek. So the locals started calling the creek "Kelly's

Mistake." The creek is steep and narrow, with heavy vegetation along the banks. In the fall of 1901, about $500 worth of gold (24 oz) was mined from this stream. But Reed thought there was "low mineral development potential due to lack of visible gold in pans."[103]

In a 1978 interview, Harry told more stories about Roshier during the time he was mining on Gold, Emma and Kelly's Mistake Creeks: "Creecy was quite a character. He was sociable. He always had a yarn to tell, you know. Creecy staked a claim on Slate Creek for awhile, brought it up to [Charles] Irish, [district commissioner]. He made out the notice himself, he wrote down, 'I claim as far as I can see across the creek and upstream as far as I can see.' [Laughter]. And he'd take it over to Irish and Irish would look at that and they'd go round and round over that. Creecy was just doin' that, I think, to aggravate Irish. He wasn't going to record it."[5]

Roshier moved from Gold Creek to Emma Creek to Kelly's Mistake and settled into a cabin there. Harry said, "He was jumpin' around all the time." Harry explained that Gold Creek was rich, and Roshier had "six or seven claims. After Creecy left [Gold Creek], I gave him $25 for two of his claims. When it rains, the creek becomes a river. One guy drowned up there before I came. Knocked him off his feet and he hit his head."[112] Harry continued to visit Roshier after he moved. "At Kelly's Mistake, Creecy had all these empty bottles hanging from the eaves of his cabin and when it rained, when the rain hit the bottles, it sounded like a piano playing. And he cut down all the trees and built these little wind mills that would go around."[132] Tishu Ulen also visited Roshier at Kelly's Mistake and commented, "In his later years he stayed in Kelly's Mistake, he had a nice little house there."[98]

In the 1940 U.S. Census, "Roshier H. Creecy" was the 106th and last person enumerated in District 4-40, the Koyukuk River Valley. Roshier's race was declared as Negro, he stated he was born in West Virginia, was sixty-seven years old, and worked fifty-two weeks a year as a placer gold miner. His notes at the beginning of the new decade relate his travels, his political views and a small moment of joy: "Arrive on Minnie Creek January 24, 1940. Leave New Deal! Broke. January 24, 1940. Got a pup April 6th 1940, 6 weeks old."

In 1941, Roshier's notes echoed a sad repeat of an earlier accident on Gold Creek. "Jack Morgan drowned and pulled out of the river by R. H. Creecy and Henry Hope August 13th 1941." Roshier had been prospecting with young Henry Hope on Myrtle Creek, where gold had been first discovered in 1898 by Knute Ellingson. Roshier wanted to poke around to see if any gold was left to find. Roshier's dog found Jack Morgan's body. According to an article in the August 15, 1941 *Fairbanks Daily News-Miner,* "They had been searching for 24 hours. The dog first sighted the body submerged in the stream. The two men started back to Wiseman to get a boat, but the mail boat of the George Black fleet came along and took the body to Wiseman."

The year of 1942 brought further tragedies. Roshier's friend, Big Jim, became ill and passed away. On September 23, 1942, Roshier lost another friend: Martin Slisco was murdered by another resident of Wiseman, Jack Welch. The September 23–23, 1942 issues of the *Fairbanks Daily News-Miner* ran the story:

Martin Slisco, 60, proprietor of the only roadhouse at Wiseman and so-called "mayor" of that settlement, was shot to death there yesterday . . . Slisco was a native of Yugoslavia and his name was Sliscovich before he became a naturalized U.S. citizen about 10 years ago. He came to Nome in the early gold-rush days as a boy, and settled at Wiseman in 1910. About five years ago he returned to Europe and brought back a young wife. They had three children . . . Welch is accused of threatening to kill both Slisco—with whom he had quarreled over a debt ($137)—and, Oliver Chappell, who had beaten Welch up a half hour before the shooting. The quarrel between Welch and Chappell was over Welch's alleged kicking of one of the Chappell's dogs which was chained up. When Chappell heard of the incident, he found Welch, and there was a fist fight, in which Welch, the smaller man, received a black eye. A few minutes later, Commissioner Irish, on the porch of his house, saw Welch go past toward his own cabin. Irish asked him what was the matter and the man is said to have replied that he was going to get a gun and kill both Slisco and Chappell. He had owed Slisco some money, and had worked for Slisco to repay the debt, but had put in seven days' work, when he believed he owed Slisco only three days' work. Irish thought it was only an idle threat when he saw Welch pass by soon afterward with a .30 caliber rifle in his hand. Irish started down the road toward the roadhouse where Welch had entered . . . Slisco looked around and asked, "What do you want?" "I want you," Welch is said to have replied, after which he raised his gun and fired, just as Slisco was getting up. With one hand clutching his chest, Slisco pushed his wife away with his other

162

hand . . . He lived half an hour. While dying, he said: "My wife, he got me. Care for my children." Meanwhile, Harry Leonard, in a cabin 50 feet away, had heard the shot and came out. At this juncture, Irish overtook Welch from behind and threw his arms around him, calling on Leonard to grab the rifle. This was done. Welch was tied up in Leonard's cabin and Leonard named to take charge of the prisoner."[133]

Welch was convicted of first-degree murder and sentenced to life in prison. The widow, Pera Slisco, moved to Fairbanks with her three children. Without Martin Slisco, Wiseman began to have a forlorn feeling. Contributing to the declining mood was the exodus of men who signed up to go to war when the United States was attacked at Pearl Harbor by the Japanese on December 7, 1941. Tishu Ulen said that's when the population of Wiseman started to decline.[98]

Roshier had been keenly following the outbreak of war in Europe, which began with Germany's invasion of Poland. Through his magazines, he was also aware of war in Asia between the Empire of Japan, which sought to dominate the Pacific, and the Republic of China. He saved a clipping from one of his magazines reporting on the conflict.

"ONCE AGAIN—AN APATHETIC WORLD LOOKS ON
WHILST TWO GREAT PEOPLES
FLY AT EACH OTHER'S THROATS. . . .
Seven thousand miles away Chinamen are dying. Seven thousand miles away Japs are lying on hospital cots—their broken bodies wracked with torture from shrapnel fragments and machine gun lead. . . .

A clipping reflective of the conflict in Asia, found among Roshier's effects after his death[21]

163

Roshier read background material on the European conflict, such as a book written in 1934 by Scott Nearing entitled *Europe: West and East*. In this book, Nearing wrote about his observations while traveling through Europe and the Soviet Union and gave his perspectives on regional economics and politics as well as fascism and Soviet communism. Nearing predicted that the conditions left behind the World War of 1914–1919 and terms of the peace treaties would cause another world war.[134]

A pacifist, Roshier was deeply troubled by the war and kept a haunting record of its devastation: "Casualties Army 106,717; Navy 35,572; Coast Guard 15,520. January 11, 1944."

As the United States entered into World War II, gold mining was severely restricted by the War Production Board. The reduction in mining activity collapsed the economic base of many towns, including Wiseman. Soon, both the store and the school in Wiseman closed.[118]

The **War Production Board** deemed gold mining nonessential and curtailed it under Limitation Order 208 in fall 1942. Miners were to focus on the recovery of industrial minerals useful to the war effort such as iron, copper and nickel. Additionally, the mining labor force and its equipment were needed in defense construction projects. Gold mine closures in Alaska were met with considerable complaint, as gold was a critical economic base to many towns; its production loss would have long-term impacts across Alaska. There were exceptions to the closure policy. For example, any placer mine that treated less than 1,000 cubic yards of material in 1941 was exempted.[86]

There was a shortage of food and supplies from wartime rationing, made worse by a large military presence.

> With the invasion of the Aleutian Islands by the Japanese in June 1942, increasing numbers of soldiers poured into the Interior. The military requisitioned supplies from businesses, exacerbating the shortage of wartime rationing. To alleviate the food shortages and to augment military access into the Alaska Territory, construction began on the **Alaska Highway**, which would connect Alaska with the continental United States through Canada's road network. Construction began in March 1942 and both the southern- and northern-end crews met in September at Mile 588 which came to be called Contact Creek. The road was built under the direction of the U.S. Army Corps of Engineers which assigned ten thousand men to the task, a third of whom were black soldiers.[86]

On September 23, 1943, Roshier wrote on a scrap of brown paper:

My moral is at low ebb.
Age has doubtless dimmed my memory somewhat.
Prejudice in the Army, Navy
and Jim Crow in this so-called democracy.
What is going on in Georgia is similar
to what is happening in Germany.

Shortly before his death, Roshier wrote a note paraphrasing a portion of the burial service from the Anglican Book of Common Prayer, derived from Genesis 3:19:

In the sweat of thy face shalt thou eat bread, till thou return unto the ground; for out of it wast thou taken: for dust thou art, and unto dust shalt thou return.

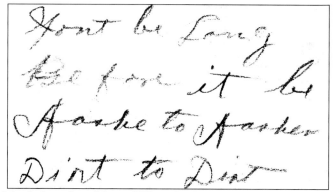

Roshier's hand-writing: "Wont be Long Before it be Aashe to Aashes, Dirt to Dirt."[21]

As the old-timers died off and the war took many men Outside, the once-vibrant Wiseman community dwindled. In the March 10, 1945 *Fairbanks Daily News-Miner* it was reported that "Before the War, Wiseman had a considerable population, composed of whites and natives. Now, most of its residents have moved away. Wiseman has only 12 white men, 1 white woman and but a few natives. White men range in age from 60 to 93, the average being about 75. Carl Frank, miner, 93; R. H. Creecy, Negro, mining on Kelly's Mistake, 78; Hans Christenson, miner, 78; Albert Nash mining on Goldstream, 76; Ace Wilcox, miner, 76; Nick Skovich, mining on Mascot, 73; Billy English, U.S. Commissioner and storekeeper, 70; Joe Ulen, radio operator and storekeeper, 68; Smith Wannamaker, mining on Nolan, 60, his wife being the only white woman. Almost all have lived there more than 40 years. They are unusually active for their ages and none lack the necessities of life, even with the airplane freight rate from Fairbanks at 12 cents a pound. Wiseman is now a camp of fine men and coarse gold. Because of its yellow metal resources, its growth and development are certain when peace comes again."

In the winter of 1948, Roshier had not been seen in town for awhile and no smoke was coming from the chimney of his cabin at Kelly's Mistake. Tishu Ulen explained what happened next: "Sammy Hope, an Eskimo friend of Roshier's, and my son, Benny, then 12 years old, hooked up eight dogs to the Yukon sled and headed to his cabin. Sammy entered the door first and seeing Creecy's body lying on the floor by the stove trying to make fire, quickly covered it with a blanket so Benny wouldn't see it. He froze to death, probably a month or 6 weeks earlier. By then he didn't have any dogs. Didn't have any wood, or dogs, had to walk. He was in his clothes." Tishu noted that mice had chewed on Creecy and a whole pile of burned block-matches lay on the floor in front of the fireless stove. He was completely out of wood. The boys loaded the frozen body on the sled; this was no easy task because one arm stretched out to the side and up over his head. When they returned to town, everyone speculated about how he died. Some thought he had a heart attack, but Tishu recalled that Roshier had been ill and walked south to Porcupine Creek from Kelly's Mistake to where the Stannich brothers, Sam and Oberin, mined. (Sam and Oberin were from Yugoslavia). Tishu said, "They were unable to help him. If he had just walked north to Wiseman, he would have been given some aid."[98] At the time of his death, Roshier was eighty-two years old.

Tishu said that Charles Irish wanted to bury Roshier wrapped only in a sheet, but the people of Wiseman vocally objected. Townsfolk built a casket out of whip-sawed lumber and built a wood fire to thaw the ground to bury him in the Wiseman Cemetery "in the middle somewhere, right alongside of Ed M. Sutphen (1856–1924) from Coldfoot." Tishu said the hole was deep enough, 6 feet. In a hushed voice Tishu confided that because Roshier's frozen outstretched arm would not fit in the casket, they had to saw it off and lay it beside him. "Charlie Irish had to give last rites. We all went to the funeral. Everybody came. Everyone liked Creecy." No marker points to Roshier's grave in the Wiseman Cemetery. "It is a big cemetery, but no crosses, nothing."[98] In a 1978 interview with Harry Leonard, Harry remembered, "Creecy was always good about having wood, but after they found him dead, I went up to his cabin and there wasn't a stick of wood anywhere."[5]

For Roshier, gold mining became the means to a life of freedom and a reason to stay among a community of people who cared for each other, regardless of race. Bobby Jones, a Nolan Creek gold miner originally from Wales, might have summed it up for a number of the oldtimers:[135]

You know, we've all been in the Koyukuk so long we're afraid to leave it. We cuss and blame the place and still we're so darn fond of it we keep on staying and digging and freezing and forking over all our dust to Uncle Sam, to get enough to eat to keep on digging and freezing and cursing the country.

Epilogue

After Roshier died, he received a letter from his older sister, Lettie Jane Trent, who lived in Lynchburg, Virginia. Joe Ulen, the Wiseman postmaster at the time, returned the letter to Lettie Jane, with a long letter dated January 9, 1949.

Dear Mrs. Trent,

I am returning your letter to your brother. I am sorry to tell you that he died at his home on a creek called Kelly's Mistake, which is down river from Wiseman. Apparently, he suffered from a heart attack and just dropped dead as he had gotten out of bed. Early in November my boy hauled a load of grub to him with a dog team and he told my boy that he would make a trip to Wiseman in 10 days or two weeks, but he never came up. After Benny (my boy) had made the trip it turned very cold and got as cold as 57 below; it stayed cold for three weeks, from 40 below to 57 below, and then when it got warmer it snowed so much that it was a hardship for anyone to make a trip anywhere. However, Sammy Hope, an old Eskimo, told me he had seen no smoke at your brother's cabin. Sammy lives across the river and two miles below and passed about a mile from the cabin. I asked an airplane pilot to circle the cabin and notice if there was any smoke or tracks and the pilot, Dick King, said there were no signs of life at the cabin. Yesterday, Sammy Hope and Benny made the trip with eight dogs, leaving here at 9:00 which is daybreak and got back at 7:30 pm, bringing the body.

They found the body on the floor where he had fallen and it was frozen, apparently he had died in November, shortly after Benny had made the trip. The U.S. Commissioner here who is also probate judge has charge of all arrangements and the estate. I don't know when the funeral will be held as the weather turned bad this morning and it is snowing hard right now as I am writing this letter. There is not much I can add except he had some claims on Kelly's Mistake Creek and a small cabin.

Other people had been on the creek before him and did not do well, but he told me once it was good. I would not know one way or the other as I never was there. It was open quite a while until he came along and re-staked it.

He mentioned to me some months ago that he did not know where his boy was. He was an old soldier and I too am an old soldier and I feel I owe it to him to write and tell you all I can. His ground is unpatented, which means that the law requires $100 labor to be performed on it for each claim. The past few years Congress suspended this work on account of miners having a hard time after the war to get started again – whether they will suspend it another year remains to be seen. I think that is all I can tell you. Now as stated before, the U.S. Commissioner had charge of his property. His address is Charles Irish, Wiseman,

Alaska. I am sorry to have to return Roshier's letter to you.

Yours truly, Joe Ulen, Post Master Wiseman, Alaska.[21]

Lettie Jane Trent wrote two letters to Charles Irish. One dated January 15, 1949 says:

Dear Sir,

I have been notified by Mr. Joe Ulen, Postmaster of Wiseman, Alaska, of the death of my brother, Roshier H. Creecy, a veteran. I would like to know how to proceed to get more information about my brother's holdings. I am aware of the government bonds purchased by him, as he told me of this and he also had money sent me at times from Washington.

Yours truly, Lettie J. Trent, Lynchburg, Virginia.[136]

Lettie Jane's second letter to Charles Irish is dated February 1, 1949 as follows:

Dear Sir,

I received the nice letter you wrote me about my brother Roshier's funeral. Thank you to the highest. I hope he left enough of something to pay you for your troubles. You asked about his father's name, it was Wyatt Creecy, his mother, Selena Creecy. They were born in Campbell County, Virginia. Roshier was born in Campbell County in 1867 [1866]. Roshier's father was in the Civil War and Roshier was in the Indian

War, but I have only seen him but once since. As for his wife and son, I don't know anything about them. I would be very glad if you would write to the War Department and find out about his bonds. He told me he bought quite a few.

Yours very truly, Lettie J. Trent. Lynchburg, Virginia.[136]

Charles Irish did write to the Treasury Department, and their response of February 17, 1949 follows:

We received your letter of January 25, 1949 in which your requested information on Roshier, who was found dead in his cabin January 8, 1949. You mentioned some checks had been returned to this office by your local postmaster and with the thought that Roshier may have owned some Series G savings bonds we made a search of our records. However, we were unable to locate a record of the purchase of any Series G bonds, and consequently are unable to reconcile your statement that some checks were returned to this office.

Chas. Peyton. Deputy Commissioner in Charge.[21]

Among Roshier's effects was found an empty envelope with a return address of Treasury Department, Division of Savings Bonds, 236 East 24th St., Chicago 16, IL. Roshier purchased savings bonds but their fate was never discovered.

Roshier's sisters wrote to Charles Irish: "Lettie Jane Trent of Lynchburg, Virginia and Mary Virginia McIver, of Mt. Hope, West Virginia, the surviving sisters of Roshier H.

Creecy, request that J. Ulen be appointed administrator of the estate of Roshier Creecy."[21] The Roshier Creecy estate was inventoried and sold as follows: "One .30-.30 rifle, $10; watch with brass nugget, $6; total $16. No inventory or appraisement was made of this estate as the property was 7 miles below Wiseman with a poor foot trail, and what property there was did not sum to be worth the expense."[21]

Harry Leonard remembered one last joke that Roshier had played: "After Creecy died, some guy wrote that Creecy said he had buried a big nugget at the end of his clothes line. [Laughter] It was gobs of gold."[5] What Harry was alluding to was a letter to Charles Irish from Cora Dubin in Woodstock, Illinois dated February 26, 1949. Cora wrote, "Remember when the plane took Mrs. Slisco and I to Myrtle Creek, left us there and went back to Wiseman? That was in 1942. Here is what she told me while we waited. She said Creecy told her he had all his bonds and money hid where no one could find it, said he had a cache in his back yard; had a wire from his door. Follow that wire and at the end was a box that didn't leak. He had all his bonds and money in it. . . Perhaps this is all more of Creecy's bull, but it could be something in it, wouldn't hurt to investigate."[21] Harry Leonard thought the story of Creecy's buried treasure was a joke. Was it? Did Charles Irish investigate and find something? We'll never know.

In 1951, Georgie Deskins died at the age of seventy-five in her daughter's home in East Orange, New Jersey. Although she died never having seen Roshier or Nathan again after they left her, she had the small comfort of occasional correspondence from them over the years.

Georgie[21]

In 1952, word reached Nathan that his father had died. In an April 2, 1952 letter from Nathan in Reno, Nevada to County Recorder's Office in Wiseman, Alaska, he wrote,

Dear Sir,

If possible can I get information on R. H. Creecy on his death. Did he have a will or any valuables. His son is asking for information.

Thank you. Yours Truly, Nathan Creastino.[21]

Harry Leonard, now U.S. commissioner, wrote back. Nathan's May 19, 1952 letter to Harry is as follows:

Dear Sir,

Thank you very much for your information about R.H. Creecy. Here I will state the hole thing. Early days Spanish American War. He married my mother she was Italian American woman just when I came in this world he left her later she devorsed him so when I got to be a young man I went out in this world to look for him so I fine him in Alaska.

I worked up there with Creecy for Joe Mathews, Rye and Jay creeks summer of 1917. I left in winter, went to Fairbanks and worked. Then, the railroad was completed to Seward the fall of 1924. I taken a trip on it then I cought a boat in Seward to the Outside never went back up there.

Mother pas away five months ago, she ask me about him, that is why I am trying to find out if he had left a will or money or valuables left to help pay bills. He made good up on Rye and Jay creeks with Joe

Mathews, 1918, 1919. I got a letter from him in February 1932, they had found some rich rock lots of it on Wild River Lake also he said that Joe Mathews died in the fall of 1931 in Tanana.

Yes I no Creecy was getting a pension from the Spanish America war vets. When I was there he had quite few dollars in safe keeping at Northern Commercial store at Bettles Alaska.

Thank you, Yours Truly, Nathan Creastino.[21]

Andy Miscovich moved into Roshier's cabin after Roshier died.[39] Harry Leonard collected Roshier's personal papers from his cabin and kept them for thirty years, until passing them on in 1978 to Joseph V. Strunka, the only person who expressed any interest in them.

In Nathan's 1978 interview about his father and their time gold mining together in Alaska, he said, "I'll tell you the truth. I would like to go back up in Alaska and go back prospecting! I would want a backhoe; I could come out with a few thousand bucks."[49] Nathan died in 1983; he was eighty-seven years old at the time of his death.

Charles Irish, in his last official notation as probate judge for the Roshier H. Creecy estate, wrote a postscript, found in Order Book No. 1, Koyukuk Recording District, Third Division:

In memoriam, Roshier H. Creecy was a unique character, given to much laughter, a lonely man, hard-working and given to much roaming around and one of those who prospected much and found little gold, as so many did. He died as he lived and alone and may God

175

rest his soul. Given under my hand and the seal of this court at Wiseman, Alaska. Charles Irish, Probate Judge.[21]

References

1. Chris Allan, *Arctic Odyssey A History of the Koyukuk River Gold Stampede in Alaska's Far North* (Fairbanks, AK: U.S. Department of the Interior, Gates of the Arctic National Park and Preserve, Fairbanks Administrative Center, 2016).

2. Mrs. Loma Pointer, Detroit MI, great-niece of Roshier Creecy, personal communications with Joseph V. Strunka from October 18, 1978 through March 19, 1981.

3. Brian Shellum, *Black Officer in a Buffalo Soldier Regiment: The Military Career of Charles Young.* (Lincoln, NE: University of Nebraska Press, 2010).

4. Fred Terrell, at Fred's cabin on Sheep Creek Road, Fairbanks, tape-recorded personal interview with Joseph V. Strunka on September 3, 1978.

5. Harry Leonard, at Harry's cabin on Archibald Creek, Wiseman, tape-recorded personal interview with Joseph V. Strunka on August 27, 1978.

6. Charlie Breck, at Charlie's cabin on Smith Creek, Wiseman, tape-recorded personal interview with Joseph V. Strunka on August 26, 1978.

7. Wyatt Creasy, Virginia death records, 1912-2014, https://search.ancestry.com/cgi-bin/sse.dll?indiv=1&dbid=9278&h=638364&tid=&pid=&usePUB=true&_phsrc=vZX1188&_phstart=successSource

8. "Weight" Creasy in the Alabama, Texas and Virginia Confederate Pensions, 1884–1958, https://search.ancestry.com/cgibin/sse.dll?indiv=1&dbid=1677&h=1079018&tid=&pid=&usePUB=true&_phsrc=vZX1191&_phstart=successSource

9. National Park Service, National Register of Historic Places, The Thomas Clairborne Creasy House, Gretna, Pittsylvania County, Virginia, https://www.dhr.virginia.gov/VLR_to_transfer/PDFNoms/227-5003_CreasyHouse_2014_NRHP_Final.pdf (accessed August 9, 2018).

10. Wyatt Creasy, U.S. Selected Federal Census Non-Population Schedules 1850–1880—Agriculture, Campbell County, Rustburgh, Virginia in 1880, https://www.ancestry.com/interactive/1276/T1132_21-00523?backurl=&ssrc=&backlabel=Return

11. Map of Campbell County, 1861–1865, Confederate States of America, Army, Department of Northern Virginia, Chief Engineer's Office, Library of Congress, https://www.loc.gov/item/gvhs01.vhs00375/ (accessed August 8, 2017).

12. George Creasy (1812–1886) Family Tree, https://www.ancestry.com/familytree/person/tree/12608774/person/202006205278/facts?_phsrc=vZX1199&_phstart=successSource

13. L. Schweikart and M. Allen, *A Patriot's History of the United States* (New York: Penguin Group, 2014).

14. Wyatt Creasy, 1870 U.S. Federal Census, https://search.ancestry.com/cgi-bin/sse.dll?indiv=1&dbid=7163&h=37620310&tid=&pid=&usePUB=true&_phsrc=vZX1203&_phstart=successSource

15. Ervin Jordan, *Black Confederates and Afro-Yankees in Civil War, Virginia*, (Charlottesville, VA: University of Virginia, 1995).

16. *Black Soldiers on the Appomattox Campaign*, "Serving the Confederacy," National Park Service, https://www.nps.gov/apco/black-soldiers.htm (accessed August 8, 2017).

17. Drewry's Bluff, "Richmond—Capital of the Confederacy," National Park Service, https://www.nps.gov/rich/learn/historyculture/drewrys-bluff.htm (accessed August 8, 2017).

18. Wyatt Creasy1880 U.S. Federal Census, https://search.ancestry.com/cgi-bin/sse.dll?indiv=1&dbid=6742&h=11962359&tid=&pid=&usePUB=true&_phsrc=vZX1204&_phstart=successSource

19. Wyatt Creasy, Virginia select marriages, 1785–1940, https://search.ancestry.com/cgi-bin/sse.dll?indiv=1&dbid=60214&h=4151880&tid=&pid=&usePUB=true&_phsrc=vZX1194&_phstart=successSource

20. India Creasey Family Tree, https://www.ancestry.com/family-tree/person/tree/12608774/person/202020832683/factson

21. Joseph V. Strunka, Fairbanks Alaska, personal holdings of notes, communications, images and documents obtained from family and friends of Roshier Creecy.

22. U.S. Army Register of Enlistments, 1798–1914, Roshier H. Creecy, https://search.ancestry.com/cgi-bin/sse.dll?indiv=1&dbid=1198&h=773274&tid=&pid=&usePUB=true&_phsrc=vZX1210&_phstart=successSource

23. *The Official Railway Guide: North American Freight Service* (Philadelphia, PA: National Railway Publication Company, 1891), https://books.google.com/books?id=6I5XgcduNQYC&printsec=frontcover&dq=editions:wifo43eIogMC&hl=en&sa=X&ved=0ahUKEwidzMb9xr7dAhUCO60KHbcXBEQQ6AEIJzAA#v=onepage&q&f=false (accessed August 20, 2017).

24. Manifest Destiny, https://en.wikipedia.org/wiki/Manifest_destiny (accessed September 1, 2017).

25. American Indian Wars, https://en.wikipedia.org/wiki/American_Indian_Wars (accessed Sept. 1, 2017).

26. A Brief History of the Buffalo Soldier, Buffalo Soldiers of the American West, http://www.buffalosoldiers-amwest.org/history.htm (accessed August 28, 2017).

27. 9th Cavalry Regiment, (April 2012), http://www.first-team.us/assigned/subunits/9th_cr/ (accessed August 28, 2017).

28. Buffalo Soldier, https://en.wikipedia.org/wiki/Buffalo_Soldier (accessed August 30, 2017).

29. Public domain images from the National Archives and Records Administration, www.archives.gov (accessed September 1, 2017).

30. Washakie,
https://en.wikipedia.org/wiki/Washakie
(accessed August 29, 2017).

31. Wyoming Places—Camp Brown,
http://wyomingplaces.pbworks.com/w/page/12714716/Camp%20Brown   (accessed August 30, 2017).

32. Lt. John Hanks Alexander,
https://en.wikipedia.org/wiki/John_Hanks_Alexander
(accessed October 8, 2017).

33. U.S. Buffalo Soldiers, Returns from regular army cavalry regiments, 1866-1916 and Returns from military posts 1806-1916,
https://www.ancestry.com/search/collections/regulararmycr/

34. David Schirer, Utah History Encyclopedia, Fort Duchesne, www.historytogo.utah.gov, (accessed September 23, 2017).

35. *Salt Lake Herald*, "Hold the Fort", December 15, 1892, Library of Congress, Chronicling America,
https://chroniclingamerica.loc.gov/lccn/sn85058130/1892-12-15/ed-1/seq-3/ (accessed August 10, 2017).

36. Uinta-Wasatch-Cache National Forest, A Century of Stewardship: Federal Troops Come to Utah, U.S. Forest Service,
https://www.fs.usda.gov/detail/uwcnf/learning/history-culture/?cid=stelprdb5052889 (accessed August 15, 2017).

37. William Dobak and Thomas Phillips, *The Black Regulars, 1866-1898* (Norman, OK: University of Oklahoma Press, 2017).

38. Gilsonite, Train Web, http://www.trainweb.org/utahrails/mining/gilsonite.html (accessed August 30, 2017).

39. Bryce Tripp, Gilsonite—An Unusual Utah Resource, Utah Geological Survey, https://geology.utah.gov/map-pub/survey-notes/gilsonite-an-unusual-utah-resource/ (accessed August 30, 2017).

40. Henry D. Styer, "Reminiscences of Ft. Duchesne, Utah 50 Years Ago," in Peter Cozzens, *Eyewitnesses to the Indian Wars, 1865-1890.* (Mechanicsburg, PA: Stackpole Books, 2001) https://books.google.com/books?id=7pSgxl_lBzIC&pg=PA421&dq=cozzens+peter+2001+ft.+duchesne&hl=en&sa=X&ved=0ahUKEwis_aLow77dAhVPhq0KHcmCD1sQ6AEIKTAA#v=onepage&q=cozzens%20peter%202001%20ft.%20duchesne&f=false (accessed August 15, 2017).

41. The Pioneer Saga of the Nine Mile Road, Duchesne County Chamber of Commerce, Roosevelt, Utah, https://www.duchesne.utah.gov/wpcontent/uploads/clerk/Nine_Mile_Canyon.pdf (accessed August 11, 2017).

42. Bonnie Dorwart, 2009. Disease during the American Civil War, National Museum of Civil War Medicine Press, 2009, www.essentialcivilwarcurriculum.com/disease-in-the-civil-war.html (accessed October 15, 2017).

43. U.S. Civil War Pension Index: General Index to Pension Files, 1861–1934, https://search.ancestry.com/cgi-bin/sse.dll?indiv=1&dbid=4654&h=1655713&tid=&pid=&usePUB=true&_phsrc=vZX1214&_phstart=successSource

44. Buffalo Soldiers, History Net,
www.historynet.com/buffalosoldiers
(accessed October 15, 2017).

45. Marya McQuirter, A Brief History of African Americans
in Washington, D.C. Cultural Tourism, D.C.,
https://www.culturaltourismdc.org/portal/a-brief-history-of-
african-americans-in-washington-dc
(accessed August 5, 2017).

46. Ron Baumgarten, All Not So Quiet Along the Potomac,
November 10, 2010,
http://dclawyderonthecivilwar.blogspot.com/2010/11/washingto
n-dc-1892-parade-of-union.html
(accessed October 31, 2017).

47. Public domain images from the Library of Congress,
https://loc.goc

48. Gustav G. Offterdinger., 1870 U.S. Federal Census,
https://search.ancestry.com/cgi-
bin/sse.dll?indiv=1&dbid=7163&h=37626685&tid=&pid=&u
sePUB=true&_phsrc=vZX1225&_phstart=successSource

49. Nathan Crestini, at his home in Reno, Nevada , tape-
recorded personal interview with Joseph V. Strunka on
October 8, 1978.

50. Brookland, Washington, D.C.,
https://en.wikipedia.org/wiki/Brookland_(Washington,_D.C.)
(accessed November 1, 2017).

51. Washington, D.C. Compiled Marriage Index, 1830–1921,
https://search.ancestry.com/cgi-
bin/sse.dll?indiv=1&dbid=60261&h=93927&tid=&pid=&use
PUB=true&_phsrc=vZX1219&_phstart=successSource

52. Nathan "Crusy" Washington, D. C. Select Births and Christenings, 1830–1955. https://www.familysearch.org/search/record/results?givennam e=Nathan&surname=Crusy&birth_year_from=1896&birth_ye ar_to=1896&count=20&collection_id=1674779

53. Klondike Gold Rush, https://en.wikipedia.org/wiki/Klondike_Gold_Rush (accessed December 5, 2017).

54. Klondike Gold Rush, National Park Service, https://www.nps.gov/klgo/learn/goldrush.htm (accessed December 5, 2017).

55. John Leonard, *The Gold Fields of the Klondike: a Fortune Seeker's Guide to the Yukon Region of Alaska and British America.* (Chicago, IL: A.N. Marquis, 1897; repr. Whitehorse, Yukon Territory, Clairedge, 1994).

56. Tappan Adney, *The Klondike Stampede*, (Vancouver, BC: UBC Press 1994; originally published 1900).

57. *Seattle Post-Intelligencer*, August 7, 1897, Library of Congress, Chronicling America, https://chroniclingamerica.loc.gov/lccn/sn83045604/1897-08-07/ed-1/ (accessed January 10, 2019).

58. Chronological Registration of Boats and Scows Passing Through Tagish, Royal Canadian Mounted Police B Division Journals, Yukon Records, R.G. 18, D4, Vol. 7, May 28 to October 22, 1898. Public Archives of Canada. C-2153. http://heritage.canadiana.ca/view/oocihm.lac_reel_c2153/3?r= 0&s=1 (accessed December 7, 2017).

59. Roshier Creecy application to join the Pioneers of Alaska, personal holding of Joseph V. Strunka, Fairbanks, Alaska.

60. Jefferson Randolph "Soapy" Smith,
https://www.findagrave.com/memorial/958/jefferson-randolph-smith (accessed December 6, 2017).

61. Kenneth Kutz, *Klondike Gold*, (Darien, CT: Gold Fever Publishing, 1996).

62. Soapy Smith,
https://en.wikipedia.org/wiki/Soapy_Smith
(accessed December 6, 2017).

63. White Pass,
https://en.wikipedia.org/wiki/White_Pass
(accessed December 6, 2017).

64. Penny Rennick, ed. *Dawson City*. Alaska Geographic series, vol. 15, no. 2, 1988. (Anchorage, AK: Alaska Geographic Society, 1988).

65. Public domain images in Wikimedia Commons,
https://commons.wikimedia.org/

66. Royal North-West Mounted Police, Yukon Territory. Report on Billeting and Traveling Expenses, Sessional Papers of the Dominion of Canada, vol. 40, no. 1, 1906,
https://books.google.com/books?id=DT9OAAAAMAAJ&pg=SL18PA49&dq=report+on+billeting+and+traveling+expenses+royal+north+west+mounted+police+1906&hl=en&sa=X&ved=0ahUKEwiw0fbowr7dAhVIX60KHXZfC94Q6AEIJzAA#v=onepage&q=Creecy&f=false (accessed December 7, 2017)

67. Mining Methods of the Klondike Gold Rush,
https://en.wikipedia.org/wiki/Mining_methods_of_the_Klondike_Gold_Rush (accessed December 7, 2017).

68. Ron Wendt, The Yukon-Klondike Gold Fields. *ICMJ's Prospecting and Mining Journal*, September 2006, https://www.icmj.com/magazine/article/the-yukon-klondike-gold fields-part-i-533/ (accessed December 14, 2017).

69. *Yukon Sun.*, "A Wild Stampede," January 17, 1899, https://news.google.com/newspapers?nid=3fE2CSJIrl8C&dat=18990117&printsec=frontpage&hl=en
(accessed January 7, 2018).

70. Report of the North-West Mounted Police for1902, https://books.google.com/books?id=GhYTAAAAYAAJ&pg=RA3PA3&lpg=RA3PA3&dq=Report+of+the+North+West+Mounted+Police+for+1902.+Printed+in+1903.+Report+on+the+Yukon+Territory+by+Assistant+Commissioner+Z.T.+Wood,+1902.&source=bl&ots=uQA1dwtu0m&sig=sK4skjKBXiO0fRY2nF3RHgMPb94&hl=en&sa=X&ved=2ahUKEwj74qiSvMPdAhUNJHwKHa5BAt8Q6AEwAnoECAgQAQ#v=onepage&q=gold%20was%20lost%20during%20the%20spring%20freshets&f=false (accessed January 19, 2018).

71. Vivian Bell, Yukon Archives, Whitehorse, Yukon Territory, Canada, personal communication email dated December 7, 2017. www.yukon.archives@gov.yk.ca

72. Georgie A. Creecy, 1900 U.S. Federal Census, https://search.ancestry.com/cgi-bin/sse.dll?indiv=1&dbid=7602&h=51318258&tid=&pid=&usePUB=true&_phsrc=vZX1226&_phstart=successSource

73. "Roshiar H. Creesy," The Territories, 1901 Canadian Census, Library and Archives of Canada, https://www.familysearch.org/search/record/results?givenname=Roshiar%20H.&surname=Creesy&gender=M&count=20&collection_id=1584557 (accessed January 18, 2018).

74. Roshier Creecy, August 8, 1903, Index of Dawson Residents, www.yukongenealogy.com (accessed January 18, 2018).

75. Angharad Wenz, Curator, Dawson City Museum. Personal communication email dated January 19, 2018, awenz@dawsonmuseum.ca

76. *Dawson Daily News*, "Koyukuk a Stayer,"August 24, 1904,https://news.google.com/newspapers?nid=9ZlFYXVOiu MC&dat=19040824&printsec=frontpage&hl=en (accessed January 19, 2018).

77. Report of the North-West Mounted Police for 1903, https://books.google.com/books?id=GhYTAAAAYAAJ&pg= RA5PA25&dq=nw+mounted+police+Yukon+1904&hl=en&s a=X&ved=0ahUKEwj409jWvOXXAhVLxVQKHX9SB9QQ 6AEIKTAA#v=onepage&q=nw%20mounted%20police%20Y ukon%201904&f=false (accessed January 19, 2018).

78. *Dawson Daily News*, "Tanana Hotel Arrivals," May 23, 1905,https://news.google.com/newspapers?nid=9ZlFYXVOiu MC&dat=19050522&printsec=frontpage&hl=en (accessed January 21, 2018).

79. "R. H. Creecy," January 4, 1906, Yukon Genealogy at Yukon Archives, Whitehorse, Yukon Territory, Canada, www.yukon.archives@gov.yk.ca (accessed January 16, 2018).

80. Hudson Stuck, *Ten Thousand Miles with a Dog Sled.* (New York: Charles Scribner's Sons, 1916).

81. James Wickersham, *Old Yukon: Tales, Trails and Trials.* (Washington, DC: Washington Law Book, 1938).

82. Agnes Burr, *Alaska: Our Beautiful Northland of Opportunity.* (Boston, MA: The Page Company, 1919), https://books.google.com/books?id=CuNCAAAAIAAJ&pg=PA215&dq=stampeders+from+dawson+to+Tanana+1906&hl=en&sa=X&ved=0ahUKEwi52ffKiarbAhUcIjQIHd6rB_wQ6AEIMjAD#v=onepage&q=stampeders%20from%20dawson%20to%20Tanana%201906&f=false (accessed April 20, 2018).

83. Fortymile, https://en.wikipedia.org/wiki/Forty_Mile,_Yukon (accessed April 20, 2018).

84. Eagle, https://en.wikipedia.org/wiki/Eagle,_Alaska (accessed April 20, 2018).

85. Circle, https://en.wikipedia.org/wiki/Circle,_Alaska (accessed April 20, 2018).

86. History of Fairbanks, https://en.wikipedia.org/wiki/History_of_Fairbanks,_Alaska (accessed July1, 2018).

87. *Fairbanks Daily Times*, "The Lavelle Young," August 21, 1906,https://fairbanksdailynewsminer.newspaperarchive.com/fairbanks-evening-news/1906-08-21/page-5/ (accessed May 15, 2018).

88. *Fairbanks Daily Times,* "Postmaster Clum Has Letters For All of These," October 29, 1906, https://www.ancestry.com/search/collections/news-ak-fa_da_ti/?name=_Creasey

89. John Philip Clum, Gold Rush Postal Inspector, Smithsonian National Postal Museum, https://postalmuseum.si.edu/gold/clum.html (accessed May 15, 2018).

90. Donald Orth, *Dictionary of Alaska Place Names*, U.S. Geological Survey Prof. Paper 567, (Washington, DC: Government Printing Office, 1967), https://books.google.com/books?id=0y48AQAAMAAJ&print sec=frontcover&dq=Donald+Orth+Dictionary+of+Alaska+Pla ce+names&hl=en&sa=X&ved=0ahUKEwjZ39X6xLvbAhU9 GDQIHSleAxgQ6AEIKjAA#v=onepage&q=Donald%20Orth %20Dictionary%20of%20Alaska%20Place%20names&f=fals e (accessed June 19, 2018).

91. Rolfe Buzzell, *History of the Caro-Coldfoot Trail (RST 262) and the Coldfoot-Chandalar Trail (RST 9)*. Office of History and Archaeology Report No. 117, (Anchorage, AK: Div. of Parks and Recreation, Dept. of Natural Resources, 2007), https://www.goldrichmining.com/media/downloads/technical_ reports/Buzzel_Chandalar_Rpt.pdf (accessed June 19, 2018).

92. Chandalar District History, Gold Rich Mining Company, https://goldrichmining.com/chandalar-gold-district/district-history.html (accessed June 18, 2018).

93. Terrence Cole, "Early Explorers and Prospectors on the Koyukuk" in *Up the Koyukuk*, ed. Robert Henning, Vol. 10 (Anchorage, AK: Alaska Geographic Society, 1983) 26–39.

94. F. C. Schrader, "Preliminary Report on a Reconnaissance Along the Chandalar and Koyukuk Rivers, Alaska, 1899" in *The 21st Annual Report of the U.S.G.S. Alaska to the Secretary of the Interior,* (Washington, D.C. Government Printing Office, 1900), http://dggs.alaska.gov/webpubs/usgs/ar/text/ar021ii.pdf (accessed January 13, 2018).

95. William Hunt, 1990. *Golden Places: The History of Alaska-Yukon Mining,* (Anchorage, AK: National Park Service, 1990), https://www.nps.gov/parkhistory/online_books/yuch/golden_p laces/chap11.htm (accessed July 10, 2018).

96. A. G. Maddren, *The Koyukuk-Chandalar Region, Alaska,* U.S. Geological Survey Bulletin 532, 1913, https://pubs.usgs.gov/bul/0532/report.pdf (accessed July 9, 2018).

97. K Capps and P. Tacquard, *The Search for Gold Along the Koyukuk River,* (Washington, DC: Bureau of Land Management, 1999), https://books.google.com/books?id=gG9XwCuXO0C&pg=PA 1902&lpg=PA1902&dq=koyukuk+mining+district+when+wa s+it+created&source=bl&ots=jNHUQgu512&sig=HqWzcC_ KcnkhbuXeYU5rGIkcLY&hl=en&sa=X&ved=0ahUKEwjOx NzP6cXbAhUICDQIHfqsBh44FBDoAQgmMAA#v=onepage &q=koyukuk%20mining%20district%20when%20was%20it %20created&f=false (accessed July 9, 2018).

98. Tishu Ulen, at 1271 9th Avenue, Fairbanks, tape-recorded personal interview with Joseph V. Strunka on March 15, 1981.

99. Bureau of the Census, *Thirteenth Census of the United States Taken in the Year 1910: Statistics for Alaska.* (Washington, DC: Government Printing Office, 1913), https://www2.census.gov/library/publications/decennial/1910/ abstract/supplement-ak.pdf (accessed May 5, 2018).

100. Alaska's Heritage: River Transportation, Alaska History and Cultural Studies, http://www.akhistorycourse.org/americas-territory/alaskas-heritage/chapter-4-9-river-transportation (accessed July 11, 2018).

101. Issues of the *Fairbanks Daily News-Miner*, personal holdings of Joseph V. Strunka, Fairbanks, Alaska.

102. History of Bettles, Alaska, Explore North Library, http://www.explorenorth.com/library/communities/alaska/bl-Bettles.htm (accessed July 20, 2018).

103. Irving Reed, *The Upper Koyukuk Region, Alaska* (Territory of Alaska: Department of Mines, 1938), http://pubs.dggsalaskagov.us/webpubs/dggs/mr/text/mr194_07 .pdf (accessed July 13, 2018).

104. Lists of Koyukuk Miners, University of Alaska, Fairbanks, Digital Library, Project Jukebox, http://jukebox.uaf.edu/gatesportal7/sites/default/files/koyukuk names.pdf (accessed July 5, 2018).

105. Wiseman and Chandalar Quadrangles, Alaska, U.S. Geological Survey, 1:250 000 (Washington, DC: USGS, 1981).

106. Robert Marshall, *Arctic Village*, (New York, NY: The Literary Guild, 1933).

107. W. Langer, *An Encyclopedia of World History*, (Boston, MA: Houghton Mifflin Co., 1948).

108. World War I, https://en.wikipedia.org/wiki/World_War_I (accessed July 15, 2018).

109. "WWI Ends" in *100 years of Alaska's Legislature: From Territorial Days to Today*, (Juneau, AK: Alaska Legislature, History, 2018), http://w3.legis.state.ak.us/100years/legislature.php?id=-3 (accessed July 15, 2018).

110. Sammy Hope, U.S. World War II Draft Registration Cards, 1942, https://search.ancestry.com/cgi-bin/sse.dll?indiv=1&dbid=1002&h=10722407&tid=&pid=&usePUB=true&_phsrc=vZX1236&_phstart=successSource

111. History of Alcohol Control in Alaska, Alaska Department of Commerce, Community and Economic Development, https://www.commerce.alaska.gov/web/amco/History.aspx (accessed June 29, 2018).

112. Harry Leonard, at his cabin on Smith Creek, tape-recorded personal interview with Joseph V. Strunka on August 30, 1978.

113. Newlyweds, Olaus and Mardy Murie, U.S. Fish and Wildlife Service National Digital Library, 1924, https://digitalmedia.fws.gov/digital/collection/natdiglib/id/7847 (accessed September 1, 2018).

114. Margaret Murie, *Two in the Far North*, (New York, NY: Alfred. A. Knopf, 1962).

115. Gold Quartz. Wiki Commons, photo by Rob Lavinsky, public domain image, https://commons.m.wikimedia.org/wiki/File:Gold-Quartz-265787.jpg (accessed September 1, 2018).

116. Copy of original transcript, Probate Court of Honorable Chas. Irish, U.S. Commissioner, Koyukuk Precinct, Alaska, 4th Judicial District, Wiseman, Alaska, on May 3, 1934, personal holding of Joseph V. Strunka, Fairbanks, Alaska.

117. Roshier Creecy, 1930 U.S. Federal Census, https://search.ancestry.com/cgi-bin/sse.dll?indiv=1&dbid=6224&h=101161529&tid=&pid=&usePUB=true&_phsrc=vZX1238&_phstart=successSource

118. S. Will and P. Hotch. *The Wiseman Historical District: A Report on Cultural Resources.* (Fairbanks, AK: Bureau of Land Management, undated), http://jukebox.uaf.edu/haul_road/assets/docs/sw_wiseman_stu dy.pdf (accessed May 5, 2018).

119. Joseph V. Strunka, Fairbanks, Alaska personal communication, August 31, 2018.

120. J. Kurtak, et al., *Mineral Investigations in the Koyukuk Mining District, Northern Alaska,* BLM Technical Report 50, (Anchorage, AK: Bureau of Land Management, 2002).

121. L. Heiner and E. Wolff, *Final Report, Mineral Resources of Northern Alaska.* M.I.R.L. No. 16. (Fairbanks, AK: Mineral Industry Research Laboratory, Univ. of Alaska, June 1968), http://dggs.alaska.gov/webpubs/mirl/report_no/text/mirl_n16.p df (accessed July 7, 2018).

122. P.S. Smith, Bulletin 868-A. Mineral Industry in Alaska in 1934. U.S. Geological Survey, 1934, http://dggs.alaska.gov/webpubs/usgs/b/text/b0868a.pdf (accessed July 9, 2018).

123. James and George Lounsbury Collection, Harry Leonard (filmmaker), still image from 8mm film, *Living and Mining Near Wiseman 1930s,* AAF-1866, Alaska Film Archives - University of Alaska Fairbanks, https://www.youtube.com/watch?v=YN0VqeW03Fo (accessed August 6, 2018).

124. Igloo History, Pioneers of Alaska http://www.pioneersofalaska.org/igloo_history.html (accessed June 12, 2018)

125. C. Naske and H. Slotnik, *Alaska: A History of the 49th State*, (Norman, OK: University of Oklahoma Press, 1994).

126. LaurieTriefeldt, "The Great Depression," *Fairbanks Daily News-Miner*, May 13, 2018.

127. George Rayburn is interviewed by Bill Schneider in Fairbanks, Alaska on March 13, 1985, audiobook on cassette, at University of Alaska Fairbanks Elmer E. Rasmuson Library, http://www.worldcat.org/title/george-rayburn-is-interviewed-by-bill-schneider-on-march-13-1985-in-fairbanks-alaska/oclc/557621509 (accessed March 20, 2018).

128. George Rayburn, vice president, at First National Bank of Fairbanks, tape-recorded personal interview with Joseph V. Strunka on January 18, 1980.

129. Dyer Anti-Lynching Bill, https://en.wikipedia.org/wiki/Dyer_Anti-Lynching_Bill (accessed July 16, 2018).

130. Vanesa Romo, African American Senators Introduce Anti-Lynching Bill. National Public Radio, June 29, 2018, https://www.npr.org/2018/06/29/624847379/african-american-senators-introduce-anti-lynching-bill (accessed July 16, 2018).

131. Campbell Robertson, "Lynching Memorial is Opening," *New York Times*, April 25, 2018, https://www.nytimes.com/2018/04/25/us/lynching-memorial-alabama.html. (accessed July 16, 2018).

132. Stories told by Harry Leonard, as recalled by George Lounsbury, http://jukebox.uaf.edu/GatesN/html/H93-15-59.htm (accessed July 5, 2018).

133. "Martin Slisco" *Fairbanks Daily News-Miner,* September 23-25, 1942, issues, personal holding of Joseph V. Strunka, Fairbanks, Alaska.

134. Scott Nearing, https://en.wikipedia.org/wiki/Scott_Nearing (accessed July 1, 2018).

135. William Brown, *Gaunt Beauty . . . Tenuous Life*, Historic Research Study for Gates of the Arctic National Park and Preserve, chap. 5, "The Civilization of the North," National Park Service, Alaska, 1988, http://www.npshistory.com/publications/gaar/hrs/chap5.htm (accessed September 20, 2018).

136. Lettie Jane Trent, Lynchburg, Virginia, Sister to Roshier Creecy, personal communication letters to Mr. Chas. Irish, Wiseman, Alaska, January 15 and February 1, 1949, original letters in the possession of Joseph V. Strunka, Fairbanks, Alaska.

Index

Matanuska Colony, **145, 146**

Mathews, Joseph "Joe" R., **85, 95, 96, 98, 105, 112, 113, 116–120, 174, 175**

McIver, Virginia, **1, 3, 6, 8, 87, 136, 144, 172**

Mertie, J. B., **137**

Miller, Frank, **128**

Moore, Norah, **126**

Morgan, Jack, **161**

Mounties (see North-West Mounted Police)

Murie, Olaus (also Mardy Murie), **113, 114**

Murphy, Jim, **112**

Myrtle Creek, Alaska, **81, 127, 128, 161, 173**

N

Nash, Albert, **166**

Nearing, Scott, **164**

Neck, Victor, **128**

New Deal, **145, 146, 157, 161**

Nine Mile Road, Duchesne County, Utah , **20, 22, 23**

Ninth Cavalry, **viii, 9–14, 18, 19, 22, 23**

Nolan Creek, Alaska (also Nolan), **xi, xii, 81, 82, 122, 127, 166, 168**

Nome, Alaska, **xi, xii, 64, 65, 69, 75, 77, 162**

Northern Commercial Store (also N. C. store), **82, 100, 101, 104, 105, 108, 141, 175**

North-West Mounted Police (also Mounties), **ix, 36, 39, 44–46, 51, 53, 65, 71–74**

Nulato, Alaska, **83, 91**

P

R

S